# ORGANISATION & COMPL

# ORGANISATION & COMPLEXITY

## Using Complexity Science to Theorise Organisational Aliveness

JACCO VAN UDEN

*Organisation and Complexity: Using Complexity Science to Theorise
Organisational Aliveness*

ISBN: 1-58112- 222-5

DISSERTATION.COM

Boca Raton, Florida

*For Pheona*

# Contents

# Introduction

The role organisations play in today's society is difficult to overestimate. Modern society is an *organised* society, meaning that every aspect of our lives is affected by organisations, one way or the other. Whether it concerns the quality of our food, our perception of conflicts in the Middle East, the infrastructure that enables us to take a walk through the park, or new ways to lodge a complaint about the government – behind it, there are organisations.

The way we think about organisations matters. Our images of organisation matter because they determine our understanding of what they are, of how they work, of what makes them tick. In this book, the focus will be on how different views of organisation lead to different interpretations of the relationship between organisation and man.

This book describes an attempt to think of organisations as *beings that live lives of their own*. The idea that organisations are living entities will be developed in contradistinction to an image of organisation that says the exact opposite, namely that organisations are lifeless objects – instruments that human beings are free to design, built, use and control. This latter view of organisation, which I will term the organisation-as-tool view, will be developed in chapter 1. In this chapter I will introduce Vitesse, a Dutch company that will be used to illustrate matters throughout this study. Vitesse is a professional football (soccer) club that according to its president needed to be transformed into a "multi-entertainment football company". I will show that a very distinct image of organisation bubbles up from the 'official' report on this process of professionalisation, one in which the Vitesse organisation is presented as a tool that Vitesse president Karel Aalbers owns and uses to realise pre-formulated goals. I will argue that this instrumental understanding of organisation is not unique to Vitesse and that the idea that organisation is a derivative – organisation follows from man's ambition to get something done – is widespread. After that I will argue that when you want to develop the contrasting theory in which organisations live lives of their own, it makes sense to see what the so-called science of complexity has to offer.

In chapter 2 I will address the question of whether or not a student of organisation is entitled to make use of the ideas and concepts that complexity scientists work with. Complexity science is often understood as the science that studies the behaviour of complex systems. I will first review the arguments of authors who maintain that organisations *are* complex systems and that we therefore have every right to apply complexity science to organisation – provided that we do so carefully. I will then contend that even when we do *not* think that organisations are essentially complex systems, and complexity science thus needs to be considered 'alien' to organisation, there is still no need to give up on complexity. I will argue that the success of complexity science in the realm of organisation does not depend on rigorous application but will ultimately be determined by the extent to which its ideas and concepts contribute to existing organisational research programmes.

In chapter 3 I will try to develop the idea that organisations are living entities by drawing from the works of authors who treat complexity science as a sophisticated continuation of 'normal' systems theory. This chapter begins with a brief introduction to the history of systems thinking in organisation studies. After that I will show that when we jump from the organisation-as-tool view as developed in chapter 1 to an organisation-as-system perspective, the human agent moves to background and stops being able to control the organisation. According to systems theorists, the organisation *itself* interacts with the environment it finds itself in. Before I actually try to theorise organisational aliveness from a systems point of view, I will briefly reflect on the epistemological aspects of that project. I will argue that I do not believe one could really prove organisations to be alive. What we can do instead is ascribe "features of aliveness" to organisations and see whether or not these "signs of organisational life" stick, so to speak. In this chapter, I will argue that organisations may come to be regarded as living entities if we manage to convince ourselves that organisations are capable of *learning*. I will then discuss the relationship between 'old school' systems theory and complex systems theory. Here the question will be addressed whether complexity theory really is the New Science it is often claimed to be or if it is just "old wine in new bottles". Chapter 3 ends with the observation that some authors reject the idea that applying complexity science to organisation necessarily requires a commitment to systems thinking. This observation is the starting point of a discussion of a theory of complexity that goes beyond the conventional systems discourse, or, at least, that pushes its limits.

In chapter 4 I will argue that a 'non-official' reading of the coming about of the Vitesse organisation shows that this organisation is not just the product of individual design; we need to acknowledge the influences of *many* parties, each of them 'moulding and shaping' the Vitesse organisation in its own particular way and for their own particular reason. At this point I will introduce Stewart and Cohen, whose theory of emergent phenomena I will rework in order to make it suitable for application in the realm of organisation. I will argue that from this point of view, the Vitesse organisation is neither the sum of its building blocks nor the outcome of a process of 'cultivation', i.e., the materialised effect of various parties trying to get the Vitesse organisation to be like other organisations.
The conclusion that the Vitesse organisation is not open to reductionist analysis sets up chapter 5, in which I describe how it can be approached instead.

In chapter 5 I will show how the work of Stewart and Cohen can be used to flesh out the concept of organisational aliveness. Given that the value of treating organisations as emergent phenomena is best determined in relation to other understandings of organisation, I will first discuss a theory that says we need to focus on the "robust qualities" of organisations. Here, "your typical organisation" is presented as a reflection of a natural order, brought about by deep laws of nature. This theory I will then contrast with a postmodern take on matters, where organisations are believed to be discursively produced and sustained. Against this background I will show that if we apply Stewart and Cohen's ideas to the phenomena we are interested in here, organisations come to be thought of as emerging from the "complicity" of multiple sources. I will argue that understood as an emergent phenomenon, an organisation is not only 'more' than that which brought it about but that it is also capable of feeding itself back into the sources from which it emerged. I will then propose to accept an organisation's capacity "to change that from which it sprung" as a sign of organisational life.

In chapter 6 I will reflect on the my attempt to use complexity science to develop the idea that organisations live lives of their own. In this concluding chapter I will compare my attempt to link complexity to organisation with the efforts of other authors on the subject. I will show that while I like complexity science for the concepts it offers to question the primacy of human agency in our thinking about organisations, most 'management thinkers' hope to find that knowledge of phenomena like emergence, self-organisation or nonlinearity can make us better organisers. I will conclude by arguing that, as I see it, complexity science compels us to admit that there are serious limits to the extent to which we can design, build and control organisations.

1

# The Organisation as Tool

## INTRODUCTION

Some believe that 11 May 1998 marks the beginning of a new era in professional football in the Netherlands. Nearly a century after its founding, "following the example of leading clubs in other countries such as Celtic, Manchester United, Chelsea and AC Milan", Ajax becomes the first Dutch football club with a quotation on the stock market. The prospectus makes clear that this move is but part of a more comprehensive programme, one that aims to render Ajax "a prominent party in the ongoing commercialisation and globalisation of professional football" (Ajax prospectus, 1998). Today, far more than being just a football club, Ajax is a company that is in the business of "football and activities related to football, such as sponsoring, advertising, media and merchandising" (see Euronext website).

According to those who feel that football is just another product, Ajax's decision to manage this product professionally makes perfect sense. But the business approach to football has not been received with applause alone – far from it. Large numbers of people (working class fans and intellectuals alike) have protested against the 'interference of business people' and the subsequent murdering of the True Spirit of Football. In his study of the history of sports, Brailsford (1991) shows that in general, any attempt to explore the profitability of sports is likely to meet strong resistance. He points out, however, that it is not so much the money *as such* that is new to sports as is the *prominence* of it. "To suppose that sport, in the ages before industrialization, had existed in some non-material world is naive. Play never took place in an idyllic economic vacuum, and by the early nineteenth century it was more than ready to begin its steady march into a full-blown business market. As far back as the early Middle Ages sport had its financial connotations, even if they went no further than the local alehouse keeper as he felt a warm glow at the approach of the annual football match and its carousing players. His successors had become sport promoters in their own right by the seventeenth century, when the Halifax publicans were mounting foot-races 'to gather the country to drink their ale'" (Brailsford, 1991: 54).

In this chapter I will describe the transformation of a Dutch football club that has wholeheartedly accepted the 'challenge' of professionalisation/commercialisation: Vitesse. In the following, as an introduction to Vitesse, I will briefly discuss the history of football, the process of football becoming a sport, the development of organised football in the Netherlands, and the (still) uncomfortable marriage between football and commerce.

## FOOTBALL

Football as we know it today was not invented as such but rather evolved into its present form. There is no straightforward answer to the question of exactly what or where football emerged from. In his comprehensive study of the development of professional football in the Netherlands, Miermans (1955) not only shows that football gradually 'liberated' itself from a mixture of general ball games, but he also points out that different studies have found the roots of football to lie in different countries. From a study of the British situation in particular, Miermans concludes that pre-modern football matches were uproarious events where muzzy young men from the lower social classes – unhindered by rules regarding playing time, number of participants or ways of preventing opponents from scoring – would battle one another to gain honour and respect. The rough nature of the game motivated regulators to ban football from the cities and by the end of the eighteenth century, football had become a mainly rural pastime (Miermans, 1955: 54).

In the 1830s, students of British public schools rediscovered football. Their teachers, rather than simply forbidding it, tried to 'tame' the game by regulating it. In its new form, football well-fitted pedagogical programmes that aimed to convert young boys into "Christian Gentlemen" (Miermans, 1955: 55). Since football was still a largely intra-school activity at that time, different schools produced different rules. This multiplicity of rules became a problem when students finished school and founded football clubs that enabled them to continue to play their beloved game. When these Old Boys tried to bring uniformity to the large numbers of rules available it became clear that the locally derived rules could not be consolidated into a single, coherent scheme. *Two* sorts of football emerged that were then defined as different sports altogether: football and rugby (modelled after the kind of 'football' that was played at Rugby School).

## Football in the Netherlands

In the 1880s, English football began to spread across the continents. Enabled by improved means of travelling, large numbers of Brits (temporarily) moved abroad, introducing their sports to the locals. In that process, thousands of British students, businessmen, workers and military men familiarized the Dutch with football, cricket, tennis and hockey. In addition, Dutch students who had studied in the United Kingdom returned to their home country with a passion for sports and persuaded their friends to join them in their games. Miermans (1955: 76) stresses that it were not just physical activities that got imported but also, and probably even more important, what sports *represented*, namely the "typical English mentality". Sports stood for something bigger. In a very real sense, the sporting ground was to be understood as an ideal micro-world and in their daily lives also, players were expected to live by the rules of the game. That is, in one's day to day business too, one should "be a sport" and subscribe to the principles of "fair play": free competition, honesty and equal chances for everyone (Hirn in Miermans, 1955: 35).

Embracing the idea behind sport as much as the game itself, boys from well-off Dutch families were unable to keep football to themselves. The liberal assumptions underlying the concept of sportsmanship – "there are no social positions on the playing field" – forced the elite to promote sports among the lower social classes, and (financially) support the latter in their founding of working class sports clubs. Catalysed by a series of mutually reinforcing developments in society, football popularised rapidly. The standard of living was improving and the working man now had both the money and time to play football. The growing popularity of football resulted in a dense network of clubs. This lowered traveling costs for players, thus making football increasingly accessible to people from the lower social classes (Miermans, 1955: 105-119). Because of the growing number of working class football players, the upper social classes began to lose their grip on the character of the game. When football was still a gentleman's sport, friends would gather to have a good time and play for the sheer joy of it. With little motivation to actually *win* the game, fair play and overall camaraderie could flourish. Popularisation put this sportive nature of football under pressure. The 'new' sportsmen played against strangers, the competitive aspect of the game regained importance, and the working man's rowdy disposition came to be reflected in how football was played. Consequently, the upper classes withdrew from football and concentrated on hockey, tennis and rugby – sports that they believed still carried within them the ideals of true sportsmanship[1] (Miermans, 1955: 122-54).

In the new situation, there was more to sportive success than just good fun or prestige. Various parties financially benefited from winning football teams: there was gate-money for the club owner, there were pubs that benefited from large crowds of thirsty supporters, there were sponsors that reaped the fruits of 'popularity by association', etcetera (Miermans, 1955: 124, 159). Naturally, the players themselves did not fail to notice that football had become an industry in its own right and began asking for remunerations. The preservers of the 'purity' of sports strongly objected to this trend. In 1909, the Royal Dutch Football Association (KNVB) states it "disapproves of [professional football], considers it harmful to the sport and the people, and will protest against it by all means necessary" (in Miermans, 1955: 149). The KNVB rejected professionalism because monetary temptations were expected to soil the minds of the players, inevitably leading to a situation in which the key features of sport would be compromised; football had to be understood as non-commercial in its very nature and professionalism would leave football just another commercial activity (Stokvis, 1979: 30). The everyday practice of football was nothing like the ideal situation pictured by the football association. In 1951 a KNVB official asserts that in the higher football divisions, "true amateurism" had become a "bombastic word, a futile thing". He advises the football association to come to terms with reality but his proposal to reconsider the "hypocritic" malediction of professional football is rejected[2]. The repercussions of the KNVB's ban on professionalism were considerable: high salaries in countries that *did* allow for professional football had attracted some of the best Dutch players, causing the quality of domestic football to drop dramatically. Moreover, because the KNVB denied players who had 'betrayed' their country the opportunity to play in the national squad, the Netherlands were of no importance in the world of international football. Eventually, the KNVB standpoint collapsed under the demand to 'loosen up'. In 1954, by majority of votes, the association formally legitimised (semi)professional football.

The founding of a professional football league did not mean that from that moment onwards football and money were considered natural partners. In their study of the history of professional football in the Netherlands, Verkammen and Vermeer (1994) point out that regrets over the loss of (the idea of) unperverted, non-commercial football have not abated with the retreat of the elite. Already in its first season, the Dutch professional football league faced a bribery scandal and in the years to follow there were recurring disputes over salaries, transfers, broadcasting rights, shirt sponsoring, mergers, and so on.

Today, sports and commerce still do not go together very well. Knowing perfectly well that football *is* business, we nevertheless act shocked when we hear two secretly videotaped Newcastle United directors ridicule fans for purchasing replica team shirts, the manufacturing costs of which are only a fraction of the £50 retail price. The very thought that there is financial side to football is only bearable, it seems, as long as the parties involved keep their business to themselves. In the Netherlands, Vitesse was one of the first clubs to radically break with this delicate understanding of the relationship between commerce and football.

## Vitesse

Founded in 1892 in Arnhem, Vitesse was everything you expected a sports club to be: a social circle of boys from the higher social classes playing games of cricket and, later, football. Vitesse was one of the first Dutch football clubs to 'go professional' but the performance of its team was all but convincing. It was not until 1971 that Vitesse made it to the *Eredivisie* (highest division), only to be relegated by the end of the season. In the following years, Vitesse became known as a rather mediocre football club that hops between the Eredivisie and the *Eerste Divisie* (second highest division). But Vitesse was not just doing poorly on the field: on the whole, things were not going very well. The appointment of a new president would change things for the better.

Local businessman Karel Aalbers decided to put an end to the misery Vitesse is in. In a documentary on the transformation of Vitesse, Aalbers describes[3] the situation as follows: "prior to my arrival, this club had gone from one deception to the other. As a consequence, there were no more than five or six hundred visitors. Vitesse was a pitiful club, a club with lots of problems, at war with nearly everything and everyone. There was nothing here, no scouting, no youth teams, nothing. The good part about all this was that from there, the only way was up. And that is where we decided we would go, basically" (Aalbers in *Werken aan Werk*, 1998). The Vitesse website summarises the metamorphosis as follows. "Under the leadership of Karel Aalbers, a new executive committee was formed that, starting in 1985, introduced a separation between professional and amateur players ... Since the introduction of the new structure in 1985, the appointment of a new executive committee and the implementation of turn-around management (the rescue operation following Vitesse's threatened bankruptcy), the continuity of policy is crystal clear. Karel Aalbers continues to be chairman of Vitesse and others from the original executive committee are still working for the club. This continuity has also reaped benefits on the pitch. Following promotion in 1989, the club continued to finish among the first five teams ... Last season, with fourth-place in the rankings, the team again qualified for European football competition. Shortly after its appointment, the new executive committee developed a policy that viewed the Nieuw Monnikenhuize stadium as inadequate to meet Vitesse's objectives. Although sporting success was one objective, there were others. Vitesse had to become a club that, increasingly, could get people to commit themselves to the team. 'Vitesse for All and All for Vitesse' is a free translation of the Dutch club motto, 'Vitesse is van ons allemaal'. Increasingly, Vitesse was playing a key role in the social lives of people. The club needed an ultramodern accommodation. In 1989, the first concrete plans were presented for a modern, multifunctional, secure, orderly and – especially – hospitable stadium. Gelredome – the embodiment of Vitesse's vision, its football vision – opened its doors on 25 March 1998 during the first match of the season against NAC (4-1)".

*✳ 1998.*

*2002-03*

*✳ a key role in the social lives of people.*

Vitesse president Karel Aalbers wholeheartedly embraced the idea that football is business. And quite successfully so: in 1999, Vitesse had a budget of almost € 27 million (compared to little over € 360,000 in 1985), it had 400 sponsors (instead of 10), it employed a full-time, 'non-players' staff of 75 (none in 1985) and sold 23,000 season tickets (versus 200). However, in Arnhem also the revolutionary did not survive his revolution and on 15 February 2000, in spite of the apparent success of *Vitesse reinvented*, "Karel the Emperor" was forced to resign as president.

## About this chapter

In this chapter, I will reflect on Vitesse's programme of professionalisation. After a brief introduction to Vitesse's new self-image, I will show that in many ways, Vitesse can be said to have taken a *Disney approach* to its business. Under the Vitesse Way, the club stopped selling 'football per se' and aimed to deliver a comprehensive experience. After a discussion of some of the products Vitesse was able to offer when it re-identified itself as a "multi-entertainment football company", I'll address the organisational implications of this move. I will argue that a very distinct image of organisation emerges from Vitesse's report on the transformation of *today's Vitesse* into the *Vitesse of Tomorrow* and the role Aalbers played in that process. In what I will call the Official Vitesse Story, the Vitesse organisation is understood as an instrument that Aalbers uses in order to realise Vitesse's mission statement. It is this organisation-as-tool view that I want to challenge in this study. My ambition is to develop the idea that organisations are not lifeless instruments but instead *live lives of their own*. At the closing of this chapter I will explain why I believe that ideas and concepts from the so-called sciences of complexity can lend a helping hand in this process.

## VITESSE: MAS QUE UN CLUB

In the brochure *Gelredome: a vision realised, an innovation by Vitesse professional football foundation*, Aalbers explains what Vitesse tries to achieve. "When it comes to our performance on the pitch, I would put it like this – we will be happy if, in a few years time, Vitesse is seen by the Dutch public as a club which is not automatically a non-starter for the Dutch title. Of course, one day we want to be the champions – I think that you have to have that ambition if you are playing at the top. Our aim is to compete for the title in the role of dangerous outsider. We will never be an Ajax, but we must get a step closer. From such a position, you can also play on the European stage. There is room for four top Dutch clubs at European level. Vitesse wants to be one of them" (Vitesse, 1998: 84). Elsewhere, Aalbers points out that Vitesse does not merely want to do well on the field. The club has "social ambitions" also. "We constantly monitor the market and we found that today's society is searching for things to identify with … Society individualises rapidly. Consequently, there is a growing need for shared experience. The success of a pop band does not depend on the quality of its songs only. It is the identification with a way of life or attitude. The same applies to football clubs. Football is no longer a minor detail of life. We are an important aspect of society. We do not just want to win the championship, although we do everything to achieve that. The ultimate goal is to make a substantial contribution to society" (Aalbers in Dutch football magazine *Voetbal International*, 1998, week 24). The Vitesse president describes that contribution as follows. "At birth, you become a member of the Vitesse-family, for which you get something in return. Vitesse needs to become part of you, it must become something sacred. To be part of something goes much further than winning or losing. This may sound a bit idealistic, but when I try to picture Vitesse in the next century, I see a value added to society" (Aalbers in regional Dutch newspaper *De Gelderlander*, 2 January 1999).

## Football redefined

Aalbers' reinterpretation of 'the business of Vitesse' has far-reaching consequences for how the club is to go about. As Aalbers sees it, Vitesse will never achieve what it wants to achieve if it hangs on to a traditional view of how to run a football club. Given that "Vitesse does not have a bulging trophy cabinet, huge bank account or national following", it needs to think and act *differently*. Aalbers puts it as follows. "One can sit and moan about the changes that currently take place in professional football[4], but we anticipated this situation. And if you do exactly that, you will find that today's problems are tomorrow's opportunities. The times are changing and that's advantageous to Vitesse. The football clubs that one sees as 'the top' because of their rich traditions cannot afford to take anything for granted anymore. Today it is all about quality of management. Everything that you see on the field is a result of policy. Vitesse and the [Gelredome] currently employ a full time staff of seventy people, all of whom are focussed one thing only: the future. We find ourselves in an ongoing process of market research and we constantly inform ourselves about developments around the world. Even now, knowing that we're sold out for next season, we do not rest on our laurels. Recently, I visited Leeds United and Chelsea Village. I have been invited by the NBA to learn about its marketing. We are always concerned with the future, and everything needs to be founded on a scientific basis. There is no royal road to success" (in *Voetbal International*, 1998, week 24). Perhaps the Gelredome stadium illustrates best what the 'New Vitesse' stands for. "Monnikenhuize, our old stadium, had great nostalgic value. But we couldn't do anything else with it. It did not give us the opportunity to attract and keep new people. The supporters we are now looking for wouldn't even dream of watching a match under such miserable conditions. But the Gelredome is an experience in itself. It is clean, friendly, safe, attractive, state of the art. You can easily get something to eat and drink, and there is something of everything to do. A completely different proposition. Of course, a Vitesse football match is still a football match, but the context has been enormously upgraded. That, coupled with the fact that football has, for a long time, been no longer the exclusive domain of men, ensures that the size of and profile of crowds at Vitesse matches will change considerably. That is not just a vain hope – it is a fact" (Aalbers in Vitesse, 1998: 84-85).

Miermans (1954: 165) argues that already at the dawn of the twentieth century, when the popularisation of football really took off, football attracted spectators who were primarily interested in being able to claim that they too "were there". Vitesse can be said to have capitalised on this phenomenon by 'turning context into content': the stuff that used to be regarded as more or less peripheral has been made a key feature of the product offer. One of the Vitesse managers I interviewed, proposed seeing Vitesse as a "*football company +*", meaning that while the football match itself remains the core activity, from a commercial point of view, the setting in which the event takes place is equally interesting. One could argue that by offering 'the very excitement of experiencing the whole thing' rather than just ninety minutes of football, Vitesse changed its business proposition from offering *sports* to selling *spectacle*, as defined by Barthes. Roland Barthes distinguishes between boxing matches (sports events) on the one hand and stage-managed wrestling games (spectacles) on the other. "A boxing-match is a story which is constructed before the eyes of the spectator; in wrestling, on the contrary, it is each moment which is intelligible, not the passage of time. The spectator is not interested in the rise and fall of fortunes; he expects the transient image of certain passions. Wrestling therefore demands the immediate reading of the juxtaposed meanings, so that there is no need to connect them. The logical conclusion of the contest does not interest the wrestling-fan, while on the contrary a boxing-match always implies a science of the future. In other words, wrestling is the sum of spectacles, of which no single one is a function: each moment imposes the total knowledge of a passion which rises erect and alone, without ever extending to the crowning moment of a result" (Barthes, 1972). Similarly, the Vitesse fan is expected to appreciate every aspect of what is presented to him or her in the light of the total proposition: the (outcome of the) football match is an important feature of why one likes Vitesse, but it does not determine that appreciation fully. Even when Vitesse is defeated, the fan should still be able to have a pleasant time. "Of course, a football club is largely dependent on the performance on the field. That will always be the case. But the more you manage to make people loyal to the club, the less you depend on results. Vitesse wants to be more than just a traditional football club, I see Vitesse as a way of bringing people together. Sporting success is a very important part of this, which is why our ambitions are so high. But that is not all. If Vitesse becomes an important factor in people's lives, that's another story. Vitesse must be worth experiencing, and the atmosphere must be right. You must feel that you really belong there, so the club's accommodation must be such that you feel comfortable and at home. If you get all these things right, your performance on the pitch is still important, but no longer a matter of life and death" (Aalbers in Vitesse, 1998: 84).

The Vitesse Way has clearly been inspired by other companies in the spectacle industry. It seems that Vitesse can justly be 'accused' of having taken a *Disney approach* to football[5]. In the following, I will briefly describe the main features of the Disney philosophy. The purpose of this section is to create a background for a more detailed discussion of the Vitesse Way.

## The Disney Way

In its very essence, Disney corporation is in the business of offering harmless entertainment for the mass: "as a consumer-driven location it is frequently beholden to the lowest common denominator. Disney strives to cater to the most number of people without being offensive or threatening" (Borrie, 1999). The Disney theme parks in particular embody the spirit of this proposition. These parks are all "about mild contentment and the over arching reassurance that there is an order governing the disposition of things", as Marling (1997: 83) phrases it. Disneyland is the place where visitors guests are assured that it's a happy, small world after all. Fred Beckenstein, senior vice-president of Euro-Disneyland Imagineering: "the whole idea is escape from reality into a place where you can simply have fun. Life is full of problems, but it is our job to stop harsh reality intruding" (Beckenstein in *Organise!*, 1999).

Disney's picture perfect world largely revolves around nostalgia. Beckenstein explains that his company is "trying to design what people think they remember about what existed". The company's ambition to enable its customers to relive their idealised childhood has materialised in an "architecture of reassurance". Disney prefers rounded intersections over ninety degree corners because the former are perceived as less rigid, less threatening, and therefore more conducive to a comfortable visitor experience (Koenig, 1994). "All these architectural and environmental touches, ranging from harmonious color schemes to the absence of garbage (a Main Street 'newspaper' was discontinued early because the discarded copies were thought to clutter the street) to the famous 5/8 building scale which 'made the street a toy,' as Disney put it, which work together to offer an accessible landscape where Disney and visitors could feel instantly 'at home'"(Vanderbilt, 1999). Disney also strives to restore the *moral* order its visitors want to remember. In Disneyland, the undesirable and threatening aspects of society are purged and visitors are encouraged to feel safe. Not only is dirt, crime and poverty removed, but social deviance is curtailed. Disney does not tolerate drug taking, unrestricted free speech, gang paraphernalia or behaviour, unusual religious practices or open displays of sexuality. People are not violent or sexual in Disneyland, unless that behaviour has been officially sanctioned. For example, the daily parade down Main Street is modelled after the many celebrations of Carnival, but without the sexual undertone. The tranquillity of the park is not to be threatened, and Disney maintains the right to ask people to leave if their appearance or behaviour might be considered offensive to other guests (Koenig, 1994; Van Maanen, 1992: 10-12).

Disney believes its employees play a vitally important role in the experience that the Disneyland visitor undergoes. The handbook of the Walt Disney World College Program reminds the student that Disney is "running a business that relies on you to bring our magic to life" (see Disney Alumni website). This requires, first of all, that employees stop to think of their jobs as labour. "Employees are coached to appear as though their work is play", Borrie (1999) writes. In Disneyland, you will therefore find *cast members* (not employees), *wearing costumes* (not uniforms), *playing their roles* (not doing their jobs) on *stage* (not out on the floor) in front of an audience of *guests* (not customers). Cast members are expected to commit themselves to a series of guidelines for Guest Service. Walt Disney World Resort business intern Kopicki (2001) explains what these guidelines look like in practice. "Seeking out guest contact means avoiding folding your arms over your chest or shoving your hands in your pockets as you may appear unapproachable. Proactively means that your make compliments such as 'That's a great shirt you've got on!' or simply informing where that Guest is from. Preservation of Magic happens when a curious parent asks 'how' Tinkerbell flies, you refrain from launching into an explanation of how a 90-pound girl gets costumed, then harnessed to a cable and pushed out of the castle window to fly across the sky into Tomorrowland. Instead you reply: 'Pixie dust'" (Kopicki, 2001). Larry Lynch, Director of Business Development at the Disney Institute, points out that cast members are also "empowered" to actively arrange for magical experiences. "One example is our program called Take Five in which cast members take five minutes out of their day to proactively do something special for a guest. We call it being aggressively friendly. Our cast members look for opportunities for magic moments–those little things that happen for guests that are utter surprises. For example, a housekeeper in one of our resort hotels discovered that a guest was not feeling well so she took the time to get chicken soup from a resort restaurant and bring it back to the guest" (quoted in Emory, 2001).

Disney offers its guests more than just a time-bound experience of nostalgia, belonging, security, or comfort. Through so called "merchantainment" Disney leads it guests to the souvenir shop, where all that Disney stands for can be wrapped and taken home as a keepsake. "Since Disney's standing policy regarding everything is to be the very best, we were taught that we do not simply 'ring up' guest purchases. We actively engage the guest, ask them about their day, if everything was found to be in order, if we can help with anything at all. The point is that it helps to create and build sales. Selling the 'Disney way' is matching the wants and needs of the Guests with the products and services that are offered. By talking enthusiastically about our products and services, a guest can be directed to a product they might need or want, but not know about. This also aids in making cherished friends" (Kopicki, 2001).

## Disneyfication

Disney probably has as many critics as it has potential guests. As Stuever (2001) sees it, "railing against all things Disney is nearly as American as a trip to Orlando. Writers deplore it. Artists mock it, and subvert its icons even in the face of desist orders from Disney's legion of lawyers. Community activists who live near Disney's financial and ecological lava flow delight in occasionally discombobulating the Disney machine. Scholarly analysis of the cultural, economic and psychological impact of Disney is now a ticket to tenure, one of the faster-growing branches of academia". Disney-bashers often accuse the company of murdering spontaneity: Disney is "smile factory" (Van Maanen, 1991) where we are forced to experience what Disney wants us to experience. The Disney business, the critical argument goes, is the business of inescapable and totalising prefabricated fun: "I hate it when I feel compelled to announce in the Pirates of the Caribbean gift shop that we are really all capitalist tools supporting a media saturated culture where we cannot buy anything without having it tied in with the latest cartoon movie having [Disney President] Michael Eisner's imprimatur. I hate it how nothing is left to chance in Disney World. I hate it that there are even signs telling the tourist where to take a picture. I hate spending any part of my vacation marveling with complete strangers about the genius of Disney crowd-control. I hate the squeaky clean staff with their professional smiles. Most of all, I hate it that my husband is forced to take me in hand and threaten dire punishment if I ruin the day for the rest of the family" (Menzies Jones, 1996).

Critique is often not limited to Disney itself. The success of the Disney Way has motivated a variety of organisations to apply the distinctive philosophy and principles to their own businesses. This process and its outcomes have been labeled the *disneyization* or *disneyfication* of society. As Vanderbilt (1999) understands it, disneyfication is "shorthand for the dreaded substitution of urban reality with a sanitized and 'Imagineered' spectacle – an opiate for the middle-class suburban masses". In a Disneyfied society, the authentic, the unguided and the sudden have made way for a homogenised culture of slavish consumption. "The 'Disneyfication' of our cities reflects a larger societal change towards the 'commodification' and 'passportisation' of experience. Today, people buy and collect 'leisure experiences' the same way they do consumer goods" (Hannigan, 1998: 33). According to Kellner, the Disney approach has been particularly 'successful' in the world of professional sports. "It appears that professional sports, a paradigm of the spectacle, can no longer be played without the accompaniment of cheerleaders, giant mascots who clown with players and spectators, and raffles, promotions, and contests that hawk the products of various sponsors". He goes on to argue that "experience and everyday life are thus mediated by the spectacles of media culture which dramatize social conflicts, celebrate dominant values, and project our deepest hopes and fears. For [French author] Debord, the spectacle is a tool of pacification and depoliticization; it is a 'permanent opium war'", meaning that the very "concept of the spectacle is integrally connected to the concept of separation and passivity, for in passively consuming spectacles, one is separated from actively producing one's life". Kellner therefore concludes that the "correlative to the spectacle is thus the spectator, the passive viewer and consumer of a social system predicated on submission, conformity, and the cultivation of marketable difference" (Kellner, 2002).

## THE VITESSE WAY

*Whatever you want*
*Whatever you like*
*Whatever you say*
*You pay your money*
*You take your choice*
*Whatever you need*
*Whatever you use*
*Whatever you win*
*Whatever you loose*

Status Quo: 'Whatever You Want'
(played just before Vitesse home games begin)

It seems safe to say that to a large degree, football has disneyfied in Arnhem. According to one of the interviewed Vitesse managers, "we are not quite a theme park, but it's a close call". Vitesse president Karel Aalbers never disguised his ambition to sell spectacle. As far as he was concerned, Vitesse had to be understood as a "multi-entertainment football company" rather than as a mere sports club. That is, instead of simply organising football matches, Vitesse makes it possible for people to "come to the Gelredome to have a fantastic night and, hopefully, to see a winning team. To use a fancy word, that's simply entertainment: to keep people busy in a very pleasant way. Football, of course, being item *numero uno*" (Aalbers in *Werken aan Werk*, 1998). In similar style to Disney, Vitesse offers the kind of experience that the majority of customers likes best. Vitesse uses monitoring devices such as customer satisfaction research surveys and customer panels to track changes in supporters' needs. "We conducted a large study to find out what day of the week the supporters would like us to play our home games. The majority of the fans preferred Saturdays. And so, next season, we play on Saturdays … Shortly, we will hire two service employees to handle complaints. Their job is to find room for improvement. We don't produce anything, we deliver a service. That is the world of Vitesse: small enough to know you, big enough to serve you" (Aalbers in *Voetbal International*, 1998, week 24).

## At Home in the Gelredome

As said, one could think of the Gelredome as the embodiment of the philosophy of the New Vitesse. "Stadium guru" Neil Gunn sees the Gelredome as an answer to the demands of a new breed of fans. "People all over the world are becoming aware of other things. Now they want what the U.S. has, ice shows like Disney on Ice, modern concessions like they've never had… [Gelredome] will provide more convenience to the public than ever before. Fans will have a lot of better feeling than in the past. They'll have access to club-seats, suites, better concession areas and a wider variety of food selections. Europeans have been wanting that" (Gunn in Vitesse, 1998: 91-2). The concept of Gelredome thus "follows the American pattern, which means that ideas such as comfort, hospitality and safety are top of the agenda. Against this background, Gelredome must become an Entertainment Home for the whole family, a convivial and pleasantly warm place, where the toilets are clean and childcare is provided as a matter of course. Where you are happy to arrive early and to hang around in a sociable environment after the event has finished. You can do this on the public promenade which runs round the complex. A meeting place for young and old with different themes and atmospheres, some of which are still being developed".

Aalbers explains that a philosophy that encourages people to feel at home is a very demanding philosophy. "The Gelredome is difficult to sum up in a few words. The overall concept is perhaps best summarized as follows: the Gelredome, a place for people. Vitesse, and therefore the Gelredome, must contribute to well-being. When you take this as your basic philosophy, you come up with completely different ideas, at the drawing board and during construction. For example, a few months ago, the toilets were built. One day, we happened to be passing, we noticed they were busy mounting the urinals. Fine in itself, but I wouldn't want such a thing at home. You can say 'feel at home in the Gelredome', but then you have to do something about those toilets" (Vitesse, 1998: 84). In Disneyland, we saw, there is nothing accidental about what the world physically looks like: small buildings, rounded corners, clean streets and so on are deliberately organised for because they contribute to a homelike feeling. Vitesse aims for something very similar, for instance through the careful use of colours in the Gelredome. Hans Ultee, who "works in the areas of colour collections, colour schemes proposals, and trend studies", and "the man behind Gelredome's colour concept" contends that "the use of colour must be reasonable, and coordinated with the purpose of a room ... The term we ultimately found for Gelredome is 'football theatre'. That is the word we geared up on. At the core of the work was the need to create a welcoming place, but for the football crowds as well as the theatre-going public. The proposal that was on the table seemed to us to create an atmosphere comparable to a comfortable hotel. That seemed to us to be going a step too far. We found it too quiet, too sedate. We discussed it in great detail, and that ultimately led to the colour concept that you now see in the Gelredome ... We based what we did on two elements; colours as creators of atmosphere and in addition a logical structure which makes it easy for people to find their way around" (Vitesse, 1998: 92).

The 'football theatre' concept also forced Vitesse to rethink what it is like to be in a *safe* place – a very important theme as football is often associated with hooliganism. "Safety coordinator" Toine Gijsbers reflects on the (potential) fruits of the *From Stadium to Theatre* project: "Vitesse's new 'football temple' is, in many ways, completely different to the many dreary stadia around the Netherlands. An important philosophy behind this fine building is to make the supporters feel at home, so they don't trash the place. And how do you make visitors feel at home? By putting on activities before and after the match, providing good catering facilities, having friendly staff, nice decoration and by letting fans watch the football unhindered by visual obstacles. This problem is removed in the Gelredome by taking away the many barriers in most stadia. In the Gelredome, not only do the fans sit close to the pitch, but there are also no high fences or deep ditches. Henceforth, fans will only be separated from the pitch by friendly stewards ... The plan was to make the Gelredome more than just a football stadium, but rather a complex to which you would like to bring the whole family. Just as you would take your family to the theatre. We didn't want a cold, bleak football stadium like so many of them. This was why we decided not to have any fences or ditches. As I said, these encourage aggression. Why do people climb fences? Because they're there! ... In the Gelredome, everyone is seated in a fresh, friendly atmosphere which does not provoke such aggression amongst fans" (Gijsbers in Vitesse, 1998: 96).

## THE COMMODIFICATION OF THE VITESSE EXPERIENCE

Vitesse's decision to switch from hosting football matches to offering a comprehensive experience has had far-reaching implications for the club's (potential) sources of income.

Gelredome has room for over twenty-six thousand visitors and prices of season tickets vary from approximately € 90 to over € 350. Given that revenues from door-money contribute significantly to Vitesse's overall turnover, one is inclined to think that Vitesse wants to sell as many tickets as possible. Aalbers explains that too much emphasis on the 'easy revenues' from admittance fees may ultimately harm the product, however. "I would rather have fifteen thousand people on a waiting list than fifty empty seats. Scarcity is the biggest phenomenon in football. Look at Barcelona, Madrid, Manchester or the Rolling Stones. Manchester United could double its capacity, but chooses not to do so because it wants to keep the fans eager". Aalbers hopes to realise something similar in Arnhem. "If you realise that your season ticket is a scanty good, you will think twice before you misbehave and run the risk of losing your season ticket ... [After riots] I saw parents and their children who hadn't been in a stadium for years, fleeing the stadium in tears. Some of them handed in their season tickets. That is when I said 'okay, no more'. Should we really accept that five hundred hooligans ruin it for twenty-two thousand other supporters? So then we decided to have season tickets holders only. These are the people who I know, who I can communicate with, who I can motivate and inform. In the end, I can reward and punish them ... The financial losses [that may result from this policy] do not outweigh the gain of stability, security and comfort" (Aalbers in *Voetbal International*, 1998, week 24).

From its own business model it thus follows that Vitesse cannot afford to rely too heavily on revenues from admission fees. Luckily, the football-based entertainment industry has been shown to offer very lucrative alternative sources of income.

## Merchandise

In the world of football, revenues from merchandise can be enormous. Take Manchester United Football Club, for example. At 'ManU', almost twenty percent of the annual turnover (some £130m in the year 2000) comes from merchandise, sold at over 123,000 square feet of global retail space. MUFC merchandise includes team wear, mugs, lamp-shades, tooth brushes, models of the Old Trafford stadium, underwear, sandwich boxes and so on. The club staffs approximately one hundred employees in its merchandising departments alone (Business Plus Magazine, 2001; Dutch national newspaper *De Volkskrant*, 22 October 1997).

Vitesse has also learned about the profitability of merchandise. "In the past we would sell a shirt or two, now we are selling € 9000 worth of merchandise. Per game!" (Aalbers in *Voetbal International*, 1998, week 24). One of the interviewed Vitesse managers points out that there are very real limitations to traditional forms of merchandising, however. He describes the situation of the Gelredome opening its doors for the same group of season ticket holders once every fortnight as a "closed market". This manager argues that "the opportunities within this setting are finite and the only way you can create more sales is by producing new merchandise, creating things that this group of people does not have yet". To overcome these restrictions, Vitesse explores the opportunities that "joint promotion" offers. In this scenario, Vitesse develops new merchandise products but rather than selling them exclusively at the Gelredome, the club approaches other companies that would like to be associated with these products. This 'third party' then sells or gives away the Vitesse merchandise. "This way you can overcome the limitations of a closed market. It allows you to realise a growth because revenues are no longer bound by your traditional environment". Still, there are only so many people to whom you can sell a product that is directly related to a particular football team. The next step in the merchandising strategy is therefore to loosen the tie between product and club. "Imagine the Tamagotchi toy has not been invented yet. Vitesse thinks it up, it has the Vitesse logo on it and everyone wants one. This would catapult you into a completely different market. To think like this, to think in *concepts*, is very difficult. But when you are already trying to serve your market in a creative fashion, you can take the next step and develop products that are interesting for other parties as well. To give an example, you could hire a photographer to shoot pictures at the Gelredome that are truly unique. You offer only a limited number of authenticated pictures for sale and people will buy these photos, not because they are photos of Vitesse but because the photos are unique. I did something similar for Lierse [a football club in Belgium]. Lierse is a village and thus a small market. We placed our product offer on the internet and we sold it to people all over the world – we even got an order from Japan. The buyers were collectors who wanted to add our product to their collections. This way of going about, global thinking, is essential if you want to grow".

In addition to offering the fans tangible merchandise items, Vitesse enables its supporters to 'live the experience' through membership of the clubs it has founded. Below I will briefly discuss the business model behind the *Vitesse Kids Club* and the *Business Club Vitesse-Gelredome*.

### Vitesse Kids Club

In the same way that the Disney Kids Club enables its members to "belong to the Magic" (see Disney website), Vitesse encourages the youngest of its fans (0 - 14 years) to become part of the *Vitesse Family* by joining the Vitesse Kids Club. Membership costs € 15 per year, in return for which the Vitesse Kids receive a Vitesse Kids Club card, newsletters and fun mail, a birthday card signed by a player and an invitation to the annual Kids Club Day. A member of the Vitesse Kids Club could be elected "pupil of the week", he or she may be selected to participate in the "flag parade" (which accompanies the players to the football field), invited to attend a training or press conference, and so on. In addition to being a product in its own right, the Vitesse Kids Club is also a platform that Vitesse uses to offer *other* products and services. One of these additional products is a paid visit by Vito, the official Vitesse Kids Club mascot. "The Vitesse Kids Club gives you the opportunity to hire Vito, an original way to make your son's or daughter's birthday a day to never forget ... Vito could do a warming-up training with the kids, participate in their games, host a prize-giving – almost nothing is too much for this young Vitesse eagle [Vito is a baby bird, modelled after the eagle in the Vitesse logo]. The Vitesse Kids Club team is more than willing to help you think of ways in which Vito can make a playful contribution to your party" (see Vitesse website).

Running a kids club can be lucrative in the long run also. The Consumer Union contends that by reinforcing certain interests and loyalties in kids, "these clubs are reinforcing interest in purchasing and loyalties to brand-name products". While kids clubs present themselves to children as "lots of fun", in selling themselves to companies that are potential advertisers, kids clubs are offered as effective ways to build customer relationships "that will last a lifetime". Kids clubs allow one to establish relationships with "the young consumers of today and the brand-loyal customers of tomorrow". More and more businesses acknowledge the blessings of this approach. Quoting from The Marketing to Kids Report, the Consumers Union reports that "many companies today, in the business of marketing to children, are reviving the kids' club theme in order to start building those happy childhood memories and warm feelings for their products. The marketing industry is realizing the importance of instilling brand loyalty at an early age, hoping it will carry through into adulthood" (see Consumers Union website; also see McNeal, 1992: 173-5). A very similar line of thought underlies the Vitesse Kids Club. As one of the interviewed Vitesse managers put it, the Vitesse Kids Club is "a breeding ground for future Vitesse fans". When these Kids grow older, "the supporters club has to follow up", thus enabling the Vitesse fan to remain an 'official' member of the Vitesse family at any stage of his or her life.

## Business Club Vitesse-Gelredome

According to Vitesse, membership of its Business Club offers much more than the opportunity to watch a game of football from a posh seat. The Business Club was designed to become a site where business people could establish new business contacts or strengthen old ones. The Vitesse website claims that the Club has been very successful in that respect. "Almost every member established contacts that paid off, sooner or later. More and more business club members visited away games. As a result, relationships emerged with business partners from other clubs. When Vitesse moved to Gelredome the business club was renamed *Business Club Vitesse-Gelredome* and it witnessed an explosive upswing to approximately 400 members. Since the move, activities have taken place in the atmospheric Gelrelounge", making the Business Club Vitesse-Gelredome "the largest and most dynamic business circuit in the Central Eastern Netherlands".

The idea behind the Business Club Vitesse-Gelredome is that its members associate themselves with the atmosphere of Vitesse/Gelredome events (football matches and other sports games, pop concerts, musicals, operas, television shows, family entertainment) and then convert that association into profitable business contacts. One of the interviewed Vitesse managers explains what he believes makes the Vitesse/Gelredome combination unique in its kind. "Karel Aalbers has been accused of building castles in the air. Well, today it is clear that he wasn't. Vitesse and Gelredome represent this – they symbolise the spirit of innovation, of taking risks, of mild aggression, of being forward". According to this manager, there are basically two reasons why businesses consider membership. "A business club supports your network, the business-to-business network in particular. Secondly, being a member of the business club gives you the opportunity to feather-bed your business partners. Vitesse and Gelredome facilitate these processes by letting your business partners want for nothing. We are willing to take this very far. Just this morning we discussed the possibility of introducing valet parking at the Gelredome. You and your business partners stop in front of Gelredome, you hand over your car keys, your car is parked for you and when you want to leave, your car is waiting for you again. Whereas the Business Club members themselves will get used to this service after a while, their business partners will be stunned ... Everything has a business potential here. Our job is to find out how this potential can be realised and extended. Our department is constantly looking for new ways to be novel, to be different".

Businesses come in many sizes and Vitesse recognises the need to make different target groups different product offers. Companies can choose between three levels of business club membership. "Business Seat holders have access to their own restaurant, the Gelrelounge, which also caters to Business Box and Business Loge holders. The latter two groups can also enter the panorama lounge, the box restaurant, where they can entertain their business contacts in a suitably high-class atmosphere". Prices vary, of course. In the 2002/2003 season, Vitesse charged a minimum of € 3100 for a business seat and € 55,500 for a business box. Business loges cost up to € 85,000 (Vitesse website; Business-Magneet, 2002).

## THE VITESSE WAY: PROFITABLE BUT DEMANDING

Now that we have an impression of the main changes that resulted from Vitesse re-identifying itself as a multi-entertainment football company, we can discuss the implications of this move for Vitesse itself. I will first show that when Vitesse decided to sell a comprehensive experience, it forced itself think of *everything* that affects this experience as "ours to manage". I will then argue that if you analyse the way Vitesse responded to the self-imposed obligation to place things under control, it becomes clear how Vitesse sees its organisation, namely as a *tool* – an instrument that the people of Vitesse are free to use as they think is right.

## Selling Total Fun: Prospects and Problems

Vitesse, we have seen, is supposed to be more than ephemeral diversion. "A football club can fill the vacuum that today's impersonal, result-driven, and individualised society has left behind. A football club has the capacity to reunite people, allowing them to share an experience. People can identify with a club. As supporters they can be part of the success; distinguish themselves from others and be part of a community", Aalbers says (in Van Mierlo, 2001: 94).

Vitesse has good business reasons for wanting to be more than just a football club. At traditional football clubs, where business success is almost fully determined by the performance of the team, poor results lead to a decline in the number of spectators, sponsoring revenues, media attention, value of players, merchandise sales, and so on. Vitesse wants to have a more robust business model, one in which a disallowed goal or a ball hitting the crossbar in extra time is *not* a matter of life and death. The Business Club Vitesse-Gelredome embodies this ambition to make overall success largely insensitive to football results. "Within Vitesse-Gelredome, the Business Club is an organisation in its own right; one that does not depend on successes of the first team. At most, the social sphere will be a slightly less cheerful. But one finds that especially under these circumstances most business deals are closed" (see Vitesse website). Business-wise, then, *Vitesse the multi-entertainment football company* has two main advantages over *Vitesse the football club*. First, whereas the business potential of football *an sich* is rather modest, there are no a priori limits to the ways in which Vitesse can milk the overall experience it aims to create. The New Vitesse simply has more (potential) sources of income, in other words. Second, by selling products that are largely immune to the performance of its squad, Vitesse spreads entrepreneurial risks over a variety of activities and thus becomes less vulnerable an enterprise.

Naturally, the lucrative business model comes with a price. When Vitesse sold football, it could consider all non-football issues more or less external. When it started offering experience, however, this not-my-business attitude could no longer be maintained because now *everything* that affects the experience matters. Under the Vitesse Way, there is much more business to mind. The New Vitesse not only needs to worry about how a player behaves during the match, for instance, it also needs to take an interest in what the player is like when he is being interviewed. The New Vitesse, more than ever more, needs to be concerned about what the press writes about the club or its president. The New Vitesse needs to show a professional interest in what it means when one of the Spice Girls puts on a Vitesse shirt during a concert *and* in how it is going to reflect on Vitesse when a camera registers the arrest of a hooligan wearing a Vitesse shirt. For the New Vitesse, the list of 'stuff to care about' is much longer than when it was a mere football club. So, in addition to being potentially very profitable, Vitesse's new business model is also very demanding: it

*creative emergence*

requires that Vitesse rethinks and redesigns almost everything. The New Vitesse does not take anything for granted. Vitesseworld[6] is a *manageable* world, one that Vitesse is free to act upon and change at will. Take social atmosphere, for example. The atmosphere in the Gelredome stadium contributes significantly to the experience of the visitor. Given that experience is exactly what Vitesse tries to sell, from its own business model it follows that Vitesse cannot afford to think of the social atmosphere as something that is already there, history-laden and fundamentally uncontrollable. The new business model forces Vitesse to take matters in its own hands and change them for the better. When a sports journalist asks Aalbers what, after years of cynicism in the old Nieuw Monnikenhuize stadium, explains the sudden emergence of a great social atmosphere in the Gelredome, the Vitesse president replies that "it did not simply emerge, it was *created*" (Aalbers in *Voetbal International*, 1998, week 24; original italics). Vitesse's mission statement serves as a guiding light in this process of rethinking and redesigning matters.

Like any other self-respecting company, Vitesse formulated a so-called *mission statement*. A mission statement is usually understood as a formal reflection on the company's very existence. It gives an answer to the fundamental question of what this company is 'here for'. As such, the mission statement works as a 'compass' that guides the actions. The Vitesse mission statement is a sketch of everything the club wants to be at some point in time. It[7] describes the expectations of Aalbers and his management team regarding Vitesse's performance in the national and international football competitions, for instance. But it also talks about the role Tomorrow's Vitesse should play in the lives of its fans, about the contribution Vitesse hopes to make to the local economy in the future, about what kind of employer Vitesse wants to be in the long run, and so on. By writing a mission statement, Vitesse created a gap between 'what is' and 'what ought to be'. As said, Vitesse believes it can only close this gap and become the Vitesse of Tomorrow if it takes a different, fresh approach to matters. Below I will discuss some of the changes that resulted from this insight.

### Relationship with Players and Other Employees

Very little stays the same under the Vitesse Way. For one thing, the fact that Vitesse moved into the entertainment industry has had important consequences for those in the spotlight. As far as Aalbers is concerned, football players are no longer simply football players. "I tell them they are the movie stars of the year 2000" (Aalbers in Dutch national newspaper *NRC Handelsblad*, 6 March 1998; also see Van Mierlo, 2001: 40).

The New Vitesse is not just interested in the performance of a player on the field. If fans appreciate Vitesse for the whole experience, then a player's *overall* behaviour becomes important. In order to make young players aware of their responsibilities as idols, Vitesse has developed a personality training course for its pupils. Head youth trainer Joop Brand explains that this so-called P-training helps young players deal with the extraordinary situation they find themselves in. "You're 17 years old and you are under a lot of pressure. Those boys find it difficult to deal with the money, the attention ... That is why we started using P-training" (Brand in *Werken aan Werk*, 1998). From the Vitesse website we learn that P-training is all about "personality formation" and that it "covers issues such as media training and dealing with fans". One of the interviewed Vitesse managers explains that Vitesse developed a formal fan mail policy in order to build and maintain a favourable relationship with fans. "Fan mail used to be sent to players directly but we found out that they hardly responded to it. So we did a test by sending players phony letters, with faked children's handwriting. Only two players replied. Now we had proof. Today, all incoming fan mail gets registered, the players make a selection ('this yes, that no'), we write the letter, the player signs it, and we send it off. Players are now held accountable for dealing with fan mail". The interviewee expects that in the future, 'sidelines' like dealing with fan mail will be formally included in a player's job description: "participation in public relations activities will be compulsory for the players". A different interviewee points out that stretching the meaning of 'what it means to play for Vitesse' can lead to conflicts of interest. "In terms of public relations, nothing beats doing things that are considered beneficial to society ... but [head coach/manager] Koeman wants players to focus on football only. There's an obvious conflict of interests there, which means that have to find some sort a balance. I told Koeman he can't blame me for wanting as much public relations as possible and send players to a hospital [to visit patients], just like you can't blame the people in the commercial department for trying to make use of players". The interviewee's latter comment makes clear that in addition to making a contribution to the overall goodwill of Vitesse, players also have a direct commercial value. Aalbers explains how their popularity can become a source of income. "Some players have a high advertising value. [Vitesse striker] Van Hooijdonk is an absolute star player, and not just on the field itself. *We* have his image rights and that offers many opportunities to our main sponsor. The amount of money the sponsor has to pay to make use of these rights is comparable to what the sponsor would spend on an entertainer. Van Hooijdonk's salary [approximately € 110,000 per month] is no different from that of players with the same status and other star players that we have. But his surplus value is determined by his image. And that's what a sponsor is looking for. We also have the image rights of Ronald Koeman. The day after [we signed Koeman] six companies informed if they could make use of his services" (in *Voetbal International*, week 8, 2000; original italics). Thus, under the Vitesse Way, players are appreciated for more than just football skills. Given that Vitesse wants to capitalise on a player's 'additional value' also, there is more about that player that matters to Vitesse, and thus more for the club to be managed. In the new situation, stuff that used to be considered *out there* and *not our business* has been reinterpreted by Vitesse as *part of the product* and therefore *ours to act on*.

The professionalisation of Vitesse has also had great impact on the jobs of 'normal' employees. Like any other football club, the old Vitesse had always depended heavily on volunteers. When Aalbers began to transform Vitesse into a real company, he replaced locals with an affectionate relationship with the club with *professionals*: individuals with an expertise in fields such as marketing and sales, finance, human resource management, communications, or the events industry. A historical interest in Vitesse, or even in football for that matter, is no longer necessary: the professionals 'simply' have to make the Vitesse Way work. As Aalbers sees it, this requires that the new employees have more than just a cold, technical understanding of what Vitesse stands for. "In this company, either the [club] colours of yellow and black get to you, in which case you don't work for Vitesse but you *are* Vitesse, or you drop out. There is really nothing in between. This company demands a lot from you. Also emotional involvement" (Aalbers in *Werken aan Werk*, 1998). So as to remind employees that they are expected to personify Vitesse, Aalbers insists that Vitesse is best understood, not so much as a company but as a *family* – Karel Aalbers being the "pater familias", of course (Van Mierlo, 2001: 28). In this respect too, Vitesse seemed to have modelled itself after Disney. According to Eliot (1993: 87), Walt Disney was the self-proclaimed father figure to a staff he had personally selected and whose members he insisted "were more like a family than employees". Boje (1995) writes that Walt Disney sold "himself as father to the 'boys' – his term for the male animators, storymen, and gag writers – and 'girls', his term for the women doing the inking and repetitive drawing work. He sold his employees the story of being 'one big happy family'". It is not hard to see the family metaphor as a refined organising principle: by 'secretly' counting on employees to respect traditional family values like loyalty, dedication or solidarity, a company can promote a work ethic that a normal employers would find very difficult to formally negotiate for. Walt Disney, for instance, used family metaphors to contest unionisation, persuading the employees to ask themselves if they really wanted to revolt against their own family (Boje, 1995).

In addition to changing relations with its employees, the New Vitesse also revised the relationship between club and *fans*.

## Relationships with Fans

We have seen that as far as Aalbers is concerned, preference for New Vitesse is ideally grounded in the fan's realisation that Vitesse, far more than being just a football club, is part of what you are. In "Vitesse Village" you go to the Gelredome to meet the rest of the Vitesse family or stay home and watch Vitesse television. You have a Vitesse bank account, a Vitesse mortgage and a Vitesse insurance, you go on Vitesse holidays, you wear Vitesse clothes, etcetera (Van Mierlo, 2001: 95). Presenting Vitesse products as tokens of a belonging to something bigger – the slogan "are you part of the family yet?" leaves little to the imagination as to how supporters are expected to think of their season tickets – can be a very profitable marketing strategy. But there are other, less straightforward ways in which Vitesse can benefit from addressing fans as members of a family.

It seems safe to argue that things were relatively simple in the old days: football was the product, the fan was the customer. Under the Vitesse Way, the distinction between 'the thing being sold' and 'the person to whom the product is sold' blurred. Earlier I showed that context became content when Vitesse started selling a comprehensive experience: the gathering of the fans, their chanting, and their being dressed in the club's kit, and their collective celebration of wins – all this is now part of Vitesse's product offer. In a way then, 'the fan' is now as much *product* as he or she is *customer*. This forces Vitesse to look after the 'quality' of the fan and make sure that the supporter functions in a way that is consistent with the overall product offer. Here, too, Vitesse uses the family metaphor. Whereas normal football clubs tend to attract (young) males, Vitesse likes the Gelredome population to reflect the composition of a 'normal' household. One of Vitesse managers I interviewed phrased it as follows: "in my view, anyone who is looking for conviviality, anyone who is looking for a day trip and who can appreciate the emotion of football can be a football supporter. A supporter is someone who wants to have everything the club can offer. A Vitesse supporter is a person who enjoys watching football and Vitesse in particular". While this manager claims to have "no problems" with the traditional, "fanatical" fan, he insists that "the family is more than that". With brochures, for instance "we carefully select the photos that we want to include. Is this an accurate representation of the Vitesse following? You will therefore find a picture of someone wearing a Vitesse shirt, but also of a sharp dressed business person, of women, of children". Vitesse has at least two good business reasons for wanting to have a heterogenous group of fans. First, different sorts of people make different target groups that Vitesse can sell different sorts of products to: t-shirts and mugs for traditional fans, Kids Club membership for the youngest of Vitesse fans, business seats and loges to companies, and so on. Second, when the Gelredome population consists of more than young men alone, the chances of outbursts of hooliganism to happen are likely to decrease. This serves the club well, of course. The authors of a research report on safety matters at Vitesse conclude that "it is reasonable to expect that when the safety partners succeed in controlling vandalism and hooliganism, this will generate more visitors and more commercial opportunities in a wide meaning of the word (sponsoring, shopping area). It will reduce the need for police force and, last not but not least, it will further improve the positive image of the professional football club Vitesse" (Ferweda, Beke and Van Wijk, 1998: 2).

According to one of the interviewed Vitesse managers, "entertainment does not tolerate hooliganism. We presents ourselves as a family business. Father, mother, son, daughter, business people: that's what makes conviviality. And that needs to be maintained at all costs – no concessions". Vitesse therefore goes out of its way to prevent clashes between rival supporter groups. Safety coordinator Toine Gijsbers: "there is an intervention team behind the scenes and, if all fails, the police. The police have also had a number of trial runs. The collaboration between Vitesse and the police is very good indeed. The golden rule for everyone is that the fans must never step onto the pitch. The grass is holy, so to speak. We are very strict and consistent about this – anyone who oversteps the mark will find his Club Card [which allows you to buy tickets] taken away. As the sanctions are so strict, fans will think twice before misbehaving because, if they do, they could find themselves banned from every stadium in the country. I don't expect fans to be that stupid" (Gijsbers in Vitesse, 1998: 96). While Vitesse does not hesitate to suppress outbursts of violence, its main ambition is to prevent them from occurring in the first place. "At the Gelredome, our aim is to treat visiting fans in a radically different way. We have already taken certain physical measures – you have to be realistic. The buses stop directly in front of the sections from where people watch the match. The sections are bordered by a separating wall made of lexaan, an apparently unbreakable, transparent plastic. Effective measures which do not affect the atmosphere in the stadium. But we want to do something much more significant. Before each home match, we will visit the supporters' association of our opponents. In consultation with them, we can decide how best to receive the visitors: stewards wearing the opponents' club colours, outlets selling our opponents' merchandise. Visiting fans will be welcomed, praised for their loyalty to their club, and so on. That is a fundamentally different approach of which we have high hopes. It fits in with the people-oriented approach of Vitesse and the Gelredome and the desire for innovation at Vitesse" (Aalbers in Vitesse, 1998: 85).

According to Ferweda, Beke and Van Wijk, Vitesse's growth has also led to an increase in the number of "unsought elements in the supporters legion". While the safety partners have come to an understanding with the 'old school' hard core fans, "the question remains whether the new breed of fans is equally manageable. It is possible that groups of people will emerge that, unlike the present hard core fans, will have very few emotional links to the club. These newcomers are much harder to control, if at all". Given that hooligans normally try to minimise chances of being arrested, it is likely that most of the problems will take place before and after the matches, outside the stadium. However, "it would be extremely unwise for professional football clubs not to take their responsibilities. The media, and thus the public, will link the violent confrontations to football and, in particular, to specific clubs. Hooliganism damages the image of a club, even if takes place outside the stadium" (1998: 1). One of the interviewed Vitesse managers explains why Vitesse cannot afford to limit its attention to the Gelredome premises only. "We have to realise that when someone wearing a Vitesse shirt causes trouble in Elst [a village near Arnhem] or in the city centre of Arnhem, people will hold Vitesse responsible for it. Supporters are associated with Vitesse. We have to account for the fact that if someone wearing a Vitesse shirt kicks up a row, that's going to affect us negatively. It causes a bad image and we don't want that ... [Hooliganism] just doesn't fit our image. Not only does it harm our own company, partners that associate with the club and the stadium will not be too thrilled about this man in a Vitesse shirt causing trouble. I am particularly concerned about how this affects our business. I want us to have a positive image because that image is much easier to sell". In addition to legal prosecution, troublemakers could also face 'excommunication' from the Vitesse family: "if we're able to find out who was making mischief, we will take measures. Hooligans in a Vitesse shirt run the risk of losing their season tickets".

But, as argued above, Vitesse prefers preventive measures over repression. In its attempt to deal with football related vandalism and violence, Vitesse seeks to establish a win-win situation by making "*controlled* concessions to the supporters", meaning that supporters can negotiate for certain rights – privileges that will be withdrawn if trust is violated. In this way, Vitesse tries to "appeal to the collective responsibility of the group" (Ferweda, Beke and Van Wijk, 1998: 3-5; original italics). Education plays an important role in the prevention of hooliganism as well. A Vitesse manager explains that club mascot Charley is not just an entertainer. The club also makes "Charley says the things we want to say". That is, Charley enables Vitesse to "educate from a third-person perspective. We teach kids that hooliganism is bad by having Charley explain this to [Vitesse Kids Club mascot] Vito". As petty as initiatives like these may appear, the manager claims that "subtle hints that Gelredome is a homely and safe place" produce effect. Even if it is only in the long run, "you'll find that people start behaving in accordance with them".

## Relationship with the Media

A final illustration of how Vitesse's self-imposed business model has forced the club to 'render things manageable' pertains to how Vitesse is portrayed in the media.

When Vitesse started offering itself as an experience that people should want to associate and identify with, the issue of what journalists write about the club became all the more important. As such, one of the Vitesse interviewees finds its most disturbing that "the trend is towards what you see in southern European countries. The commercial aspect has become more prominent: it is all about headlines, everything must be sensational". The interviewee contends that as a result of this development, articles on Vitesse are sometimes of rather poor quality. "For instance, in an informal setting I mentioned a situation that I find somewhat strange: a photographer has free access to the Gelredome and takes pictures of the product we deliver. However, if we want to use the pictures taken by that photographer, they charge us for it. So, still in this informal setting, I tell them that we'll have to see where we are going with that situation. Next day, [national Dutch newspaper] *Algemeen Dagblad*: 'Vitesse to Deny Admittance to Photographers' ... We discussed the issue with the NSP [the association of Dutch sports journalists] but their investigation was inadequate. *De Journalist*, a journal for professional journalists, publishes on the matter but tells one side of the story only, not ours. I talked to them about it [and since] all our arguments were right, they had nothing to say for themselves. Never heard a thing about this whole issue again. But the damage was already done". The interviewee criticises the lack of professionalism among some members of the press: "good journalists have their stories checked by Vitesse before they publish it because they don't want to blunder. But if you ask [some journalists] if you can read an article before it goes to print, they give you a lot of grief. They immediately feel assaulted". The interviewee asks himself a rhetorical question: "why can't we criticise journalists? A club has to put up with everything, supposedly. We are the first to oppose to this ... We are trying to find out the best way to deal with this matter. Can we defend ourselves? Should we get angry over and over? Should we respond at all? And if we do, should we do so in that same newspaper? Or should we start using our own, competing media? And will these competing media be taken seriously in the long run? ... Maybe it is best to tell some of the journalists, and this option was discussed just yesterday, 'look, you take some interest in what goes on at Vitesse, you do a little writing, but how do you really go about? You're a sensationalist. From now on, you are welcome to attend the matches but that's it. No press officer to give you a hearing, no press hour, no access to the training site. Nothing. Just like you don't have access to the premises of [Vitesse sponsor] OHRA seven days a week'. Then all sports journalists would be upset. But the current situation is also far from ideal. We have carried out a boycott – that's what they called it; we didn't call it a boycott, but referred to it as somewhat more restrained press services, not pro-active anymore. For a while, we were on non-speaking terms with some newspapers. If they don't do their homework properly, then neither will we. Should we really be serviceable to a newspaper that doesn't get its facts right?".

A Vitesse manager explains that the club has answered the question of how to communicate with the press in three different ways over the years: "we started out with really no policy for dealing with the press whatsoever. Then came a service model of utter servitude, basically. Partly due to the club's growth we are now ready to take the last step in the process of professionalisation: a firm grip and a well-balanced dose of service". The interviewee explains that as a result of this change in policy, it has become harder for journalists to get to talk to Vitesse president Karel Aalbers. "Karel used to be the spokesman but we deliberately put restrictions on the ease of access to him. We did so for a number of reasons. One is that we wanted to relieve the president of some of his duties – he simply does not have the time to do it anymore. Furthermore, reduced accessibility to the president, through carefully selected interviews, makes it easier to adequately communicate the Vitesse philosophy. And it has to do with prestige: 'you can't just talk to the president!' It is part of the professional image that we want to communicate ... You don't get to talk to Swelheim [president of Nuon, Vitesse's main sponsor] every day, do you?". I believe that the recurring references to other *companies* rather to other *football clubs* hold significance for they make clear how Vitesse wants to be seen: Vitesse thinks of itself as a normal company and finds that it is no more than reasonable for the press to treat it accordingly, like a normal company. Journalists that *do* understand that Vitesse is more than a football club are praised for doing so: "[a particular journalist] is among the good ones. He knows what we're trying to do here. He sees the big picture and understands Vitesse from a business economics perspective. Because he operates on a higher level, it is easier to talk to him".

Thus, like 'the personality of players' or 'the behaviour of fans', 'representation in the media' is something that the New Vitesse forced itself to consider manageable. That is, given that the way in which Vitesse is portrayed in the media affects the experience that Vitesse tries to sell, the club simply cannot afford to wait and see what the press writes – its own business model compels Vitesse to try and influence it.

## A Summary of the Vitesse Way

The Vitesse Way can be summarised as follows. When Karel Aalbers was appointed president of Vitesse, he essentially reinterpreted the very *sort* of the business Vitesse was in: Vitesse was no longer to be thought of as a football club but rather as a 'multi-entertainment company' that sells a comprehensive experience to families. The New Vitesse sketched an ideal version of itself and the gap between the *Vitesse of Tomorrow* and *Vitesse in its current form* created room for action. At the same time it was concluded that the Vitesse of Tomorrow, as captured in the mission statement, could never become reality if Vitesse was to hold on to 'how things were done in the old days'. First of all, it was necessary that all that was taken for granted when Vitesse was still a football club was critically reviewed and re-conceptualised in the light of the newly adopted business discourse. The New Vitesse stopped seeing things that were 'just like that' and rendered the many elements of Vitesseworld fundamentally manageable: the fan was replaced by the 'pleaseable' customer, the volunteer of whom you can only be appreciative made way for a professional who can be instructed, coverage by the media changed from being 'out of our hands' to 'ours to influence', and so on. Having assured themselves that Vitesseworld is theirs to act on, the people of Vitesse then set out to effectuate the Vitesse Way: now that we have committed ourselves to posing a constant threat to the traditional top 3 in Dutch professional football, we must invest in our scouting apparatus; and given that we want to offer our fans an ongoing experience, we must develop merchandise products that supporters can take home; and given that the audience appreciates Vitesse for more than just results on the field, we must see to it that the overall behaviour of the players is in order, etcetera, etcetera.

In what I will refer to as the *Official Vitesse Story* from now on, there is a strong causal relationship between, on the one hand, 'what things are like in Vitesseworld' and 'the mindful actions of the people of Vitesse' on the other. That is, if we look at the way the New Vitesse presents itself (in the media, in its own brochures, in interviews, on its website, on television, etcetera) one notices that the club is deeply convinced of its capacity to create its own world. As far as the New Vitesse is concerned, everything you see in Vitesseworld is the result of policy – the effect of deliberate design, creation and maintenance. In Vitesseworld things are what they are, not because they *are* like that but because they have been *made* like that: everything is a reflection of how Vitesse organised things. Or rather, as the Official Vitesse Story constantly reminds us, is a reflection of how *Aalbers* organised things.

## VITESSE IS AALBERS

The Official Vitesse Story sends out a very clear message: had Aalbers not been appointed president, then Vitesse as we know it would never have come about. The brochure *Gelredome: a vision realised, an innovation by Vitesse professional football foundation*, for instance, suggests it was really Aalbers' vision that was realised. Aalbers is presented as 'one of the two founding fathers of Gelredome', as 'fantastic, not a fantast', as the man who 'learns from the mistakes others make', as someone who 'had the strength to paddle upstream for ten years' and 'one of the few individuals who can link leadership to vision', as 'that persistent Vitesse president who deserves extra credit for making his dream come true', as the one capable of 'mobilising business partners to raise money', as the 'engine behind the ongoing professionalisation of Vitesse', etcetera (Vitesse, 1998: 22-79). It was a local business man with a "black and yellow heart" who came to Vitesse, who saw what needed to be done, and who conquered the world of football-based entertainment. Ergo the nickname "Karel the Emperor".

In telling a story of almost miraculous success, Vitesse, again, looks very much like Disney. "Walt Disney studios is an organization founded on storytelling. It is a very successful story-manufacturing and story commodification business", Fjellman (1992) writes. In the same way that the Gelredome stadium is Officially understood as a product of the genius of Karel Aalbers, Disney tells the story that Mickey Mouse, the character on which the Disney empire was built, was born from the hands of no one but Walt Disney himself. "A struggling young artist, he (Walt) had befriended a family of mice that took up residence in a waste-paper basket. One particular mouse had, reputedly, become so tame it would climb up onto Walt's drawing board to be fed on scraps of food". In 1948, Walt recalled how

Mickey Mouse "popped out of my mind onto a drawing pad 20 years ago on a train ride from Manhattan to Hollywood at a time when business fortunes of my brother Roy and myself were at a lowest ebb, and disaster seemed right around the corner. Born of necessity, the little fellow literally freed us of immediate worry. He provided the means for expanding our organization to its present dimensions and for extending the medium of cartoon animation towards new entertainment levels. He spelled production liberation for us" (Boje, 1995; Holliss and Sibley, 1988; Marin, 1983; see *Walt Quotes* at Disney website). Dave Iwerks contends that this precious story has very little to do with the actual course of events. Iwerks, son of Disney's former business partner Ub Iwerks, points out that "it's pretty clear now that Mickey was Ub's character. Even the [Disney archives] concede that Ub created Mickey, although their version has it that Walt stood over Ub's shoulder when he did it. The whole scenario of the train story the studio used to be so fond of is just not right at all" (in Eliot, 1993: 36). Arnhem has its own Mickey Mouse story. One of the most impressive features of the Gelredome is its retractable pitch, a world-wide premier. According to the Official Vitesse Story, "the idea of a telescopic pitch arose in a conversation between Vitesse chairman Karel Aalbers and building contractor Gert Bruil, whose building company with the same name forms a part of the building consortium. Both men love a good cigar. While they were trying to light their cigars, a half-opened matchbox fell on the floor. Both men suddenly thought, 'that's how we'll do it,' and a world first was born" (Vitesse, 1998: 92). Van Mierlo, however, points out it was one of the technicians involved in the Gelredome project who came up with the idea of a retractable field. Aalbers, not a technician, was unable to fully grasp the concept and the matchbox example was used to visualise the underlying principle. The image works for Aalbers and the matchbox becomes an important showpiece for him. Aalbers lectures the blessings of the retractable playing field over and over, up to the point where he identifies himself with the very concept (Van Mierlo, 2001: 70).

By itself, the question of who really invented the sliding pitch is of no real importance here. The matchbox anecdote is significant because of what it stands for, namely the Official suggestion that, in the end, everything about Vitesse comes down to Aalbers. When an interviewer asks Aalbers if it is a good thing that people often associate the name of the football club with that of its president, Aalbers explains this "perception" as follows. "When I became president in '84 … we started a rescue operation and made plans for a new stadium. That was quite a revolution. In fact it was so pioneer that everyone had something to say about it. So you're in the spotlights. If, in addition, you see that club progressing step by step, no matter from what angle you look at it, that makes me the figurehead". The Official Vitesse Story carefully communicates that, of course, Aalbers could not have done it alone and depends on the help of others. "I am merely the conductor standing in front of the orchestra. But I can't even play the violin. I need to have fantastic musicians" (in local Dutch newspaper *Haagsche Courant*, 7 November 1998). Aalbers, in other words, needs to be understood as a *leader*. Aalbers understands Vitesse as "a pyramid" and he sees it as his task to see to it that "that spark, that vision that comes from above, is widely agreed upon" (Aalbers in *Werken aan Werk*, 1998). Aalbers – "the Johan Cruijff of football club presidents", according to his right hand Hein Rood – initiates, plans and oversees the paving of the Vitesse Way.

To be able to keep up his good work, Aalbers believes he needs a great deal of freedom. "In the world of football, it is all about swift and adequate action. Suppose I can buy a player in Romania. Imagine if I would have to make a call to some buffoon [someone to supervise financial processes at Vitesse] to see if we have a couple of grands to spare. I'd make a fool of myself". Elsewhere, when explaining Vitesse's stormy success to representatives of the Japanese football league, Aalbers argues that "a successful football organisation requires a captain with the mandate to make decisions after he has studied the pieces of information that his management-specialists presented to him. Of course, he is supervised by the board of directors and, from a greater distance, by the supervisory board, but these institutes should never stand in the way of adequate management" (Aalbers in Van Mierlo, 2001: 12, 111).

In the Official Vitesse Story, it is Aalbers who saw what was wrong with Vitesse, it was Aalbers who saw what needed to be done and it was under Aalbers' supervision that appropriate action was taken. So while the Vitesse president should not be mistaken for a tyrant – his management team does not see him "as a dictator, but as an inspirator" (Aalbers in *Voetbal International*, week 8, 2000) – the Official Vitesse Story makes clear that Aalbers, and Aalbers only, has the final say: "if Karel doesn't want it, it is not going to happen", as one of the interviewed managers described the situation.

## THE ORGANISATION OF VITESSE

As a student of organisation, I am particularly interested in the image of organisation that emerges from the Official Vitesse Story. The formal report on the professionalisation of Vitesse insists that the Vitesse of Tomorrow will be the product of deliberate design, creation and maintenance. That is to say, nothing good will happen unless Aalbers et al actively *organise* for Vitesse's mission statement to become reality. Organisation is the mother of Vitesse's future success. The particular image of organisation that the Official Vitesse Story puts forth is perhaps best visualised by means of an analogy. It seems that Aalbers thinks of himself as a sculptor who looks at a boulder (*Vitesse today*) and believes he can transform it into a wonderful piece of art (*the Vitesse of Tomorrow that the mission statement describes*). After having assured himself that the boulder lends itself to being worked on (*Vitesseworld is rendered fundamentally manageable*), the sculptor then determines what actions he has to take to get from the raw material to the end product and decides what specific chisels (*a professional work force, the founding of a business club, the Gelredome, etcetera*) he will use to actualise the imagined piece of art. If we follow this analogy, Aalbers thus has a very instrumental understanding of the Vitesse organisation: the Vitesse organisation is the tool that Aalbers deliberately chooses to use in order to realise the Vitesse of Tomorrow. As far as Aalbers is concerned, only he himself knows how to use the Vitesse organisation correctly. "I frequently ask myself the question if my being president is still in the best interest of Vitesse. Not long ago I seriously considered taking a step back, but the reality was that many people at Vitesse would have gotten into trouble. Only a few are capable of keeping the ship dry at this level", as Aalbers describes the situation (in national Dutch newspaper *De Telegraaf*, 28 October 1999). The fact that the Karel Aalbers was forced to resign in February 2000 makes clear that not everyone agreed that Aalbers was indispensable.

According to the spokesman of Vitesse's supervisory board, the discharge of Aalbers was induced by "different opinions about priorities in the realisation of the club's ambitions. The supervisory board could no longer agree to the speed at which and the way in which Karel Aalbers wanted to carry out policy". Aalbers had a very different reading of the story. In his opinion, it was daylight robbery: "a gun was put to my chest" (in *Algemeen Dagblad*, 19 February 2000). Financial compensation for the stolen Vitesse organisation is not an option: "one million, six million, a tenner. It's nothing. I don't want money. I want my club back". While Aalbers grieves over his personal loss ("I feel like the father whose entire family was blown away. I have nothing left"), his *real* concerns are for Vitesse. To give some idea of the significance of his involuntary resignation, Aalbers suggests that "maybe this is to Vitesse what the plane crash was to Manchester", referring to the accident in which eight Manchester United players lost their lives in a plane crash. Aalbers is not only convinced that the promise of Tomorrow's Vitesse will never be fulfilled now that the sculptor is gone, what is even worse perhaps is that by taking out the artist in the middle of the process, the work in progress is bound to disintegrate. "They don't know what they're doing, they are destroying a wonderful piece of work", "my club is going to pieces", and "by sending me away, nothing will hold. Total breakdown threatens". Aalbers' immediate return is of greatest importance because "the heart was cut from the club. The philosophy flows away. I feel responsible for that" (Aalbers in Van Mierlo, 2001: 160-1; in *Voetbal International*, week 8, 2000; in *Algemeen Dagblad*, 23 February 2000). If one thinks of the Vitesse organisation as an instrument, then Aalbers' loss must be some other party's gain – theft requires both a victim *and* a thief. In the eyes of Aalbers and his followers, it was clear who took the Vitesse organisation from its rightful owner: the "greedy energy farmers" of Nuon. Vitesse's shirt sponsor "carefully staged an antisocial coup" and stole the Vitesse organisation, only to use it for the realisation of its *own* goals (Vitesse's head of communications Hein Rood in local Dutch newspaper *Arnhemse Courant*, 17 February 2000).

The fact that the Official Vitesse Story needs to introduce a third party to account for the fact that the organisation is still 'there' after Aalbers was removed, brings us to the assumption that I am especially interested in: understood as a tool, an organisation does not have, or could ever have, a life of its own. It is this assumption that I want to question in this study.

## Organisations: Lives of their Own

For this study, Vitesse is interesting, not so much in itself, but for what it stands for. The Official Vitesse Story essentially says that "organisations are there because we use them to get something done". This is an all but exceptional understanding of organisation. I believe that it is safe to say that organisations are generally regarded as *derivatives*, meaning that when we see organisations, we automatically go looking for people and goals to explain and justify their existence.

There is a common belief that organisations cannot do without organisers. We have seen that when the Vitesse organisation continued to exist after organiser Aalbers was forced to step down, the Official Vitesse Story restored the conceptual order by introducing a *new organiser*; a new party to own and control the organisation. The same principle applies when the goals that initially legitimised the organisation are no longer available. If an organisation continues 'to be' in spite of the fact that the original goals have already been reached or are simply no longer relevant, then we assume there must be *new goals* that give the organisation a reason to be. Take Greenpeace, for instance. "In 1971, motivated by their vision of a green and peaceful world, a small team of activists set sail from Vancouver, Canada, in an old fishing boat. These activists, the founders of Greenpeace, believed a few individuals could make a difference. Dave Birmingham raises Greenpeace sail on Phyllis Cormack. Their mission was to 'bear witness' to US underground nuclear testing at Amchitka, a tiny island off the West Coast of Alaska, which is one of the world's most earthquake-prone regions. Amchitka was the last refuge for 3000 endangered sea otters, and home to bald eagles, peregrine falcons and other wildlife. Even though their old boat, the Phyllis Cormack, was intercepted before it got to Amchitka, the journey sparked a flurry of public interest. The US still detonated the bomb, but the voice of reason had been heard. Nuclear testing on Amchitka ended that same year, and the island was later declared a bird sanctuary". After the initial goal was realised ("the voice of reason had been heard"), the Greenpeace organisation did not cease to be. But if the Greenpeace organisation no longer exists to help people bear witness to US underground nuclear testing at Amchitka, what, then, explains and justifies the 'being there' of the Greenpeace organisation? Similar to Vitesse, that introduced a *new organiser* to account for the ongoing existence of the Vitesse organisation, Greenpeace solved the existential crises of its organisation by thinking up *new goals* that the Greenpeace organisation can help realise. The Greenpeace website points out that since the Amchitka 'success', the

Greenpeace organisation has been used to try to put an end to hazardous exports and trawl fishing, to protest chlorine bleaching, to start a "genetically engineered food fight", and so forth. And so the Greenpeace organisation still has a reason to be. "Today, Greenpeace is an international organisation that prioritises global environmental campaigns" (see Greenpeace and Greenpeace USA websites).

What is significant of the Vitesse and Greenpeace examples is that in both cases, the organisation is assumed a passive object; at all times, the organisation belongs to an external organiser who uses it for some, equally external, reason. The goals may change and an organiser may be replaced, but the assumption that an organisation is there to mediate between man and his ambition goes unquestioned. It is exactly this fundamental assumption that I want to take on in this study. In this book I want to develop the idea that organisations, far from being tools that we can use at will, *live lives of their own.*

In order to elaborate on the idea that organisations are living entities I will turn to the complexity science discourse and think of organisations as "complex systems" or "emergent phenomena". As I will show, this move has quite far-reaching consequences. For instance, understood as a tool, an organisation does not amount to anything in the absence of an outside organiser. As soon as we start thinking of organisations as complex systems or emergent phenomena, on the other hand, they become capable of organising themselves, of "self-organisation". Moreover, according to the organisation-as-tool view, organisations are what we want them to be and do what we want them to do. When we rethink organisations through the language of complexity, however, they come to display not-designed-for or "emergent" properties.

By challenging the very assumptions that underlie an instrumental understanding of organisation, the science of complexity seems highly supportive to the development of the idea that organisations have lives of their own. But does this line of argument work? Do the ideas and concepts of complexity science really apply to organisation? Can we really rethink organisations through the language of complexity? And what are the benefits of actually doing so? What exactly will change if we stop to think of organisations as tools and start treating them as complex systems or emergent phenomena instead? And, the most important question, what precisely does 'applying complexity to organisations' contribute to the project of rendering organisations living beings? These are the issues I want to address in this book.

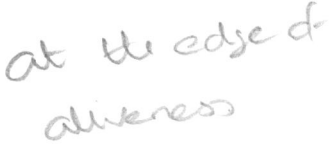
at the edge of
aliveness

2

# On the Relation Between Complexity Theory and Organisation

## INTRODUCTION

One of the first books on complexity science I read was Stuart Kauffman's *At Home in the Universe* (1995), the jacket notes of which insisted that Complexity is more than just another theory: "a major scientific revolution has begun, a new paradigm". Insistence on the revolutionary nature of complexity research turned out to be characteristic of many books on the subject matter, as Medd and Haynes (1998) also found: "what these books have in common is the claim that the age of classical science, with its emphasis on mechanistic determinism, equilibrium, and stability, and its positivist and reductionist methodology, is at an end ... A paradigm shift or a scientific revolution is being witnessed, they claim". The prophets of Complexity Science maintain that our dawning understanding of the nature of complex (adaptive) systems will change the very way in which science is conducted. In other words, what we are dealing with is nothing less than a *New Science* – a Science that is to replace the hegemonic Newtonian paradigm completely and will, as such, "affect the lives of everybody on the planet" (Brockman, 1995: 19).

A great deal of the excitement over the works of complexity theorists appears to follow from the claim that complexity science transcends the disciplines of academia. Kauffman's discovery of "order for free", for instance, is not just relevant for the world of molecules and cells – Kauffman is a biologist – but is also said to hold significance for our understanding of the origin of life itself, the rise and fall of great civilisations, culture, and giant corporations (Kauffman, 1995: jacket notes). The hope that every single field of research will benefit from the New Science is widespread. Complexity scientists' revolutionary discoveries "could change the face of every science from biology to cosmology to economics", Waldrop maintains (1992: jacket notes). Roger Lewin has even less reservations. As he sees it, complexity science is a "revolutionary technique [that] can explain any kind of complex system – multinational corporations, or mass extinctions, or ecosystems such as rain forests, or human consciousness" (Lewin, 1993).

Many students of organisation have accepted the promise of complexity science. "Business organizations are also complex adaptive systems. This means that what complexity scientists are learning about natural systems has the potential to illuminate the fundamental dynamics of business organizations", Regine and Lewin write (2000: 6). The list of specific ways to apply complexity science to organisation seems endless: Olsen and Eoyang (2001) believe that the "emerging paradigm" of complexity has important consequences for the work of "change agents", Sanders (1998) applies "complexity to strategic thinking – the most essential skill in today's fast-paced business environment", Wheatley (1993) discusses what the New Science means for leadership, Stacey (1996) appreciates complexity for its capacity to challenge the "mental models" of management, and so on.

According to some, the proliferation of books that attempt to apply this "entirely new, unified way of thinking" to organisation and management poses a real problem (Waldrop, 1992). Bill McKelvey, for instance, senses that "complexity science applied to management" has all the earmarks of becoming a management consulting fad (1999). Together with Steve Maguire, McKelvey has therefore sought to differentiate between sound applications of complexity theory on the one hand and reckless ones on the other. As guest editors to a special issue of *Emergence: A Journal of Complexity Issues and Management*, Maguire and McKelvey aim "to give readers a broad overview of the general quality of complexity applications to CEO problems and to test how vulnerable to faddism they are" (Maguire and McKelvey, 1999: 19). This special issue contains fifty reviews of over thirty books on the relationship between complexity and management.

In the following section I will derive from their "overall summary of the total message that emerges from the reviews", Maguire and McKelvey's basic understanding of the relationship between the science of complexity and organisations. I will show that the authors believe that organisations really *are* complex systems and that, as such, there must be more to the application of complexity than 'mere metaphor'. I will then argue that the New Science of complexity is perhaps not entirely new and that, especially in the light of the ambition to develop a common language for seemingly different phenomena, it makes sense to compare complexity science to cybernetics.

## THE GRAND COMPLEXITY PROJECT

Like the reviewers whose findings they summarise, Maguire and McKelvey are troubled by what they regard as the lax treatment of complexity theory. "Not unexpectedly, the complexity gurus are most upset with how complexity science terms are loosely, if not metaphorically, defined and tossed in managerial discourse – one goes as far as to suggest that the book offers many insights for managers but one should simply black out all references to complexity science ... other reviewers worry about 'loose definition' and applications, 'oversimplification', 'incorrect use of concepts', 'superficial' treatments, lack of research, and missing the computational modeling underlay of complexity science" (1999: 55). According to Maguire and McKelvey, sloppy applications make it impossible to fully exploit the potential of complexity science. "From what the reviews indicate, as well as our own reading of the trade books, the New Science is well on its way toward short-lived faddism unless serious research shows that there is more than metaphor to chaos theory and complexity science applications" (1999: 57). Maguire and McKelvey are not alone here. Michael, Michael and Rebecca (1999), for instance, write that "it is our belief that the complexity sciences offer an approach to the understanding of social change that has more than metaphorical or analogical benefits". Similarly, like Johnson and Burton (1994: 320), who believe that the metaphorical use of complexity theory is "problematic", Fuller and Moran assert that "moving beyond metaphor" is important because when "there is no grounding of these analogies in [the world of small firms], there is no evidence that complexity has validity in describing or explaining empirical observation" (1999: 50).

The reason why Maguire and McKelvey believe that the relationship between organisations and complexity theory is not just metaphorical becomes clear when we think through the authors' reference to "the particular complex systems that are human organizations". Apparently, as far as Maguire and McKelvey are concerned, organisations are but a particular kind or sub-category of complex systems. And when organisations essentially *are* complex systems, a theory of complex systems simply *is* a theory of organisations. The ideas and concepts from the science of complexity thus *literally* apply to organisation. According to Maguire and McKelvey, complexity science gets to the bottom of organisations and allows us to know these phenomena as they really are, in and by themselves. By understanding the relationship between complexity theory and organisations this way, Maguire and McKelvey firmly locate themselves in the 'complexity school' that says that in the case of complex systems, differences between different sorts of phenomena are but skin-deep only: if you scratch the surface, you will find phenomena as diverse as ecologies and brains work in the same sort of way. The reason for this is as simple as it is important: different phenomena "work in the same sort of way because they are the same sort of system" (Byrne, 1998: 53). Logically then, these so-called 'different' phenomena can all be explained by whichever theory it is that describes the "sort of system" that they essentially are. As far as Meiss (2000) is concerned, this is one of the "most exciting aspects" of complexity theory, namely that it "has applications to a wide variety of fields, from mathematics, physics, biology, and chemistry, to engineering, economics, and medicine" and thus "brings researchers from many disciplines together with a common language". Complexity scientists are not the first group of researchers to get excited over the promise of shared scientific language, however.

## The Ideal of a Common Language.

Young (1990) points out that many scientists have tried to reduce the number of academic discourses and find a single language to discuss both social and natural phenomena. "Comte thought that sociology could find the laws of social dynamics. Laplace held that modern science was powerful enough to predict social phenomena with precision were all initial states and all laws of interaction known; he assumed linearity. Pareto said: 'My wish is to construct a system of sociology on the model of celestial mechanics, physics, and chemistry'". Probably the most rigorous and systematic attempt to arrive at a scientific lingua franca was made during the Macy conferences, held shortly after World War II.

The idea behind the Macy conferences was to "bring together a group of researchers working on the forefront of their fields to forge a new interdisciplinary paradigm that became known, retrospectively, as cybernetics. Christened by Norbert Wiener, cybernetics was conceived as a science that would develop a common explanatory framework to talk about animals, machines, and humans" (Hayles, 2000: 246). According to Bale, the "introduction of cybernetics as an interdisciplinary field led to considerable enthusiasm among the scientists who attended the Macy conferences. Many ... believed the ideas offered were sufficiently deep, yet acceptably overarching, that out of them might come a vocabulary suitable as a unifying conceptual framework for the biological and social sciences" (Bale, 1995). The hope of finding a single discourse for a wide range of phenomena rested on the assumption that these various phenomena were essentially all "information processors that encoded and decoded messages, exacerbated or corrected their actions through feedback loops, and demonstrated causality" (Hayles, 2000: 246). In Wiener's own words: "it is my thesis that the physical functioning of the living individual and the operation of some of the newer communication machines are precisely parallel in their analogous attempts to control entropy through feedback. Both of them have sensory receptors as one stage in their cycle of operation: that is, in both of them there exists a special apparatus for collecting information from the outer world at low energy levels, and for making it available in the operation of the individual or of the machine. In both cases these external messages are not taken neat, but through the internal transforming powers of the apparatus, whether it be alive or dead. The information is then turned into a new form available for the further stages of performance. In both the animal and the machine this performance is made to be effective on the outer world. In both of them, their performed action on the outer world, and not merely their intended action, is reported back to the central regulatory apparatus. This complex of behavior is ignored by the average man, and in particular does not play the role that it should in our habitual analysis of society; for just as individual physical responses may be seen from this point of view, so may the organic responses of society itself. I do not mean that the sociologist is unaware of the existence and complex nature of communications in society, but until recently he has tended to overlook the extent to which they are the cement which binds its fabric together" (Wiener: 1948).

## Cybernetics and the Grand Complexity Project

There are at least three interesting parallels between cybernetics and complexity science as introduced above. First, the research programmes of both complexity theory and cybernetics are founded on the assumption that the phenomena under study can safely be stripped of their earthly forms and discussed on a more fundamental, more abstract level. Second, on both occasions it is believed that 'higher level knowledge' can be shared among researchers from all sorts of disciplines. Third, the language of the 'hard', natural sciences is favoured over that of the social sciences.

Cybernetics was based on the idea that machines and living individuals are in essence information processors. Complexity theorists, on their turn, believe that when you look carefully, you will find that while many phenomena *appear* to be different, they are, in reality, all complex systems. *If* such a shared 'complex systemness' indeed exists and *if* it allows itself to be studied and known, then the resulting theory of complex systems would be of great significance. The assumption that phenomena as diverse as earthquakes, ecologies, brains, cultures, economies, languages or organisations are all complex systems allows for the following situation to be conceived. A student of the particular complex system that is an ecosystem carries out research and 'uploads' his findings into a big database where knowledge about complex systems is stored. That piece of knowledge then becomes available to other students of complex systems. It may prove useful for the student of the particular complex system that is the brain, for example. If the latter researcher is not so much interested in the superficial 'brainness' of her research object as she is in its underlying, more fundamental 'complex systemness', then she will be able to profit from the knowledge that the student of the particular complex systems that are ecosystems has decided to share with his fellow students of complex systems. Under what I will call the Grand Complexity Project, complexity scientists working in all sorts of faculties are free to exchange research findings – including those students who work in the faculty of Management and Organisation. "Yes, we said 'exchange'. As that field within the social sciences that devotes itself to the study of 'organization' and 'organizing', it would be surprising if management and organization studies had nothing to contribute to complexity scholars as they turn their attention to systems composed of human agents" (Maguire and McKelvey, 1999: 24). Byrne agrees and maintains that all complexity scientists are created equal. He insists that even though complexity research as we know it has its roots in the 'hard' sciences, the insights offered by 'soft' scientists are no less valuable: "in no sense whatsoever is the project of applying the ideas of complexity theory to the social driven by any sort of physics envy ... It is true that chaos/complexity emerges from the experimental mathematics and thermodynamics, and has been particularly developed in physical chemistry and evolutionary biology. But, and it is a big but, once the social sciences get going, then other fields of inquiry will have a lot to learn from them" (Byrne, 1998: 17). There are important conditions that need to be met before students of complex systems can actually learn from one another. For one thing, the exchangeability of research findings requires that complexity researchers mind their language. For the results of research on the particular complex system that is a human organisation to make any sense to the student of the particular complex system that is an ecosystem, it is necessary that these research findings do not contain references to organisation. That is, were a student of human organisation to include in his final conclusions concepts like strategy, culture, leadership, technological developments or budgets, then the data would be useless to ecologists. Knowledge of the particular complex system that is an organisation thus needs to be stripped of its organisationness before it can be offered to the community of complexity researchers. Luckily, this can be arranged for under the Grand Complexity Project. As argued above, the fundamental presumption that underlies this Project is that the differences that normally encourage us to distinguish between organisations, economies, languages or coral reefs are of no fundamental importance. Hence, we can safely forget about earthly forms and focus on the deeper complex systemness.

But if not in the language they normally talk about organisations (strategy, culture, leadership, technological developments, budgets) how are students of organisation to communicate their research findings instead? Here, too, there are important parallels between complexity theory and cybernetics. Norbert Wiener left no room for misunderstanding as to what he thought an unifying conceptual framework for discussing various sorts of information processors had to look like: "cybernetics is mathematics or it is nothing" (Wiener quoted in Hayles, 2000: 148-9). The participants of the Grand Complexity Project share this preference for the language of the hard sciences. As Byrne (1998: 55) sees it, complexity science can only deal with "mathematically formalised accounts of reality". Mathematics offers 'lean', abstract descriptions and thus has a natural advantage over any language that offers 'thick' descriptions – descriptions that *do* make reference to the specifics of the situation from which the knowledge was derived. Knowledge that is embedded in time and place does not lend itself to being uploaded into computers. According to

Maguire and McKelvey that is a real problem, given that "complexity science and computational modeling go hand in hand". To overcome the problem of descriptive thickness and to do away with context, Maguire and McKelvey propose alternative concepts to describe organisational life. Typical organisational phenomena like "conversation elements, people, departments" are rendered "stochastically idiosyncratic agents", because the "platform assumptions" of agents "are more easily tolerated in computational models" (1999: 56). The advantages of converting persons, conversions or departments into agents are clear for as e.g. Krogh (1996) points out, "an agent may be anything". The concept of agent is an extremely 'tolerant' concept in that it hardly denies anyone or anything the opportunity of being one. And this suits the participants of Grand Complexity Project well: whereas staff meetings, managers or the human resource management department mean nothing to the student of the ecological complex systems, he *can* make use of the work of the student of organisation who publishes on the behaviour of stochastically idiosyncratic agents.

The Grand Complexity Project can be summarised as follows. Seemingly different phenomena may not be all that different. A New Science suggests that all natural systems are complex systems which implies that they can all be explained by an entirely new, unified way of thinking: complexity theory. This complexity theory assumes that complexity researchers can exchange their gathered knowledge of complex systemness and that the common language for doing so is the language of mathematics.

## PROBLEMS WITH THE WAR ON FADDISM

Now that we have some basic understanding of the kind of the complexity science research programme Maguire and McKelvey propose, let us look at how these authors think that the fact that complexity science is still a "nascent" discipline affects the work of students of organisation. According to Maguire and McKelvey, "if complexity researchers themselves have not yet reached a consensus on how to integrate and synthesize all the ideas and concepts they bring together from diverse disciplines it would appear unwise for organizational researches to charge ahead with the building of models or entire organization theories and management philosophies, drawing a few concepts from one discipline and a few from another based on whatever is convenient or has a nice metaphorical ring to it" (1999: 56, 25). This recommendation raises at least two important questions: who are these 'complexity researchers themselves' and how likely is it that they will ever reach consensus?

One problem I have with Maguire and McKelvey's call for reserve pertains to their reference to the group of 'complexity researchers themselves'. This reference appears very much at odds with the main presumption underlying the research project Maguire and McKelvey seek to participate in. Almost by definition, the Grand Complexity Project leaves no room for the *a priori* identification of a distinct group of complexity researchers: anyone who has good reasons to believe that his or her research object is a complex system is, or can be, a complexity scientist. In fact, by recommending that organisational researchers sit still until complexity scientists have finished their business, Maguire and McKelvey create a distinction between complexity scientists on the one hand and organisational researchers on the other – a dichotomy that is logically inconsistent with the authors' earlier reinterpretation of students of organisation as students of "the particular complex systems that are human organizations". Moreover, by maintaining this distinction, Maguire and McKelvey seem to inadvertently deny that a student of organisation is as equal a partner in the exchange programme of the Grand Complexity Project as any other complexity scientist.

Perhaps a more fundamental problem is the following. Maguire and McKelvey believe it is possible for complexity scientists to reach "a consensus on how to integrate and synthesize all the ideas and concepts they bring together from diverse disciplines". I think it is safe to say that the chances that such mass consensus will ever be reached are nil. Like any other field of research, the science of complexity consists of large numbers of 'rival schools' that battle one another over issues as fundamental as what complexity really is, over the way in which complexity is to be studied, over how complexity concepts should be applied, and so on.

good. ✓

## A Variety of Theories of Complexity

The Grand Complexity Project I sketched above is exactly the kind of research programme that compels organisation theorist Robert Chia to warn against the dangers of introducing complexity theory to the realm of organisation. Chia insists that "contrary to the populist notion of a science of complexity with established immutable principles designed to deal with ever-more complex configurations of relations in both the natural and social world, it transpires that the basic premise of a science of complexity is the *systematic and deliberate descriptive reduction of the complexes of human experiences into a transmittable and understandable form*". He argues that complexity scientists engage in "a deliberate programme of simplification in which the vague complexes of sense-experience are systematically compressed and converted into a conventionally recognizable and accepted form of discourse". Whereas in the eyes of Chia the qualification 'complex' always follows from how an observer *experiences* a phenomenon, the complexity researcher takes as his subject matter an "objective complex state of affairs existing independent of the observer systems". Chia is probably right to conclude that "much of the literature on complexity ... treats the latter as a stable and external condition". Still, by snubbing complexity science completely on the basis of what many complexity scientists have to say, Chia throws out the baby with the bath-water. Complexity science is more than the Grand Complexity Project he dislikes so much (Chia, 1998: 344-6; original italics)

As Chia sees it, because of the work of complexity scientists, "chaos is now reconceptualized as extremely complex information" (1999: 343). From that conclusion onwards, Chia no longer feels the need to differentiate between chaos and complexity and dismisses the science of complexity, using the same kind of arguments Gibson Burrell uses to protest chaos theory. "Beware of chaos theory and catastrophe theory for they tell us that it is possible to understand major changes by using mathematics, so they are by no means symptomatic of the forces for uncertainty. In fact these theories, despite their titles, are the last vestiges of modernity. That chaotic and catastrophic changes are in principle understandable would have been the everyday view of heroic figures in the 1960s organization theory" (1996: 657). Some complexity scientists appear to agree with Chia that there is no reason to discriminate between complexity and chaos. Byrne (1998) and Phelan (1999), for instance, make references to "the language of chaos and complexity" or "the adherents of the theories of chaos and complexity (hereafter 'complexity theory')", thus suggesting that complexity and chaos are basically the same thing. But Hayles argues that while the concepts are related, complexity and chaos are *not* the same. She defines chaos as "complexity's kissing cousin" (Hayles, 1999a). Cilliers also believes there is a difference: "the hype created by chaos theory has abated somewhat, but the perception that it has an important role to play in the study of complex systems is still widespread. Although I would not deny that chaos theory could contribute to the study of complexity, I do feel that its contribution would be extremely limited" (Cilliers, 1998, ix). Marion shows that the relationship between complexity and chaos is subject to much debate. "Many argue that Chaos Theory is a general theory of nonlinear dynamics and Complexity Theory is a subset of Chaos. Some would argue just the opposite, and yet others see little to distinguish the two. Another school of thought maintains that Chaos and Complexity are two sides of the same issue … To make things even more confused, complexity has meaning within Chaos Theory that differs from our definition of it. Edward Lorenz argues that the term *complexity* is often used interchangeably with Chaos, but that it is sometimes used in a specialized sense to refer to irregularity in space while Chaos refers to irregularity in time. Alternatively, complexity may refer to the length of a set of instructions required to depict a system". Marion himself has yet another outlook on the matter: "I argue, however, that Complexity, while exhibiting characteristics of Chaos, is nonetheless distinct from it. The two share general nonlinear premises, yet they represent different phenomena … Complexity is a hybrid state between stability and Chaos [,] the thin transition zone where stability ends and Chaos begins" (Marion, 1999: 5, 23; original italics).

57

The overall disagreement on the relationship between complexity and chaos is exemplary of a more general phenomenon, namely that complexity science is anything but a coherent and internally consistent theory that can be criticised *as such.* In the following I aim to show that, if anything, the science of complexity is an ongoing debate between different schools representing different 'versions' of complexity science. In the process, it should become clear that because of the great differences between these various versions of complexity science, there is little hope that complexity scientists will ever reach consensus over what complexity really is and how it is to be approached – something Maguire and McKelvey believe is needed before students of organisation can apply complexity in the first place.

*Reflexivity ...*

Chia's spurn of the science of complexity is largely informed by his assumption that complexity scientists do not recognise that the label 'complex' has everything to do with human experience. Chia assets that complexity scientists take 'the complex' as an objective reality, open for unbiased research. While some complexity researchers indeed assume that an objective account of complexity can be formulated, quite a few others agree with Chia that complexity is *not* a given state of affairs. Disagreement over the question of whether or not the observed phenomenon is 'contaminated' by the observer's role in the investigative process is also a theme that links the science of complexity to cybernetics.

Participants of the aforementioned Macy conferences disputed vigorously over the role the researcher played in the cybernetic model. Hayles shows how a technical discussion about *homeostasis* led to a more fundamental discussion about the position of the observer. She writes that the "homeostasis constellation developed in relation and opposition to another constellation centered on reflexivity. Through the idea of the feedback loop, homeostasis had already built into it the notion of circular causality... Applied to language, circular causality opened up a passage into the dangerous and convoluted territory of reflexivity, for it implied that an utterance is at once a statement about the outside world and a reflection of the person who uttered it" (Hayles, 2000: 147). Van Pelt argues that during the 1952 Macy conference, "the dueling paradigms of homeostasis and reflexivity met head to head over the issue of scientific objectivity. The dominant group of intellectuals, including the neurophysiologist Warren McCulloch (credited as one of the fathers of the neural net), propounded an idea of information founded on assumptions of a detached observer safely distanced from the observed". The strongest objection against the ideal of an objective theory of information was probably formulated by hard-line Freudian psychoanalyst Lawrence Kubie who, as Van Pelt puts it, sought to "insert subjectivity into the debates defining information as universally portable, disembodied data" (Van Pelt, 2000). Hayles contends that the "association of reflexivity with psychoanalysis meant, for many of the participants,

58

that the concept was a dead end that had little or no scientific value. Not only could it not be quantified, it also subverted normative assumptions about scientific objectivity ... if reflexivity was to be credible, it had to be insulated against subjectivity and presented in a context where it had at least the potential for rigorous (preferably mathematical) formulation" (2000: 149).

The researcher-researched relationship was as awkward an issue to those involved in the cybernetics project as it is to today's students of complexity. Indeed, as Chia argues, there are complexity scientists who believe that 'complex systemness' exists, independent of our noticing it. Byrne, for instance, found that "linearity and order seemed to be being forced on a world which really isn't like that, but I didn't have the vocabulary for doing more than worry. They were flashes of light on the way to the sunrise of complexity theory". For Byrne, in other words, complexity simply 'is' – it is an inherent feature of the world: "the complex is real" (1998: 3, 37). Understood as an outer reality, complexity becomes accessible for the formal, 'cold' language of mathematics. By and large, this is what Byrne believes the study of complexity should be all about: "chaos/complexity involves both quantitative measurements and the development of mathematically formalised accounts of reality based on those measurements – the twin essentials of any quantitative programme of scientific understanding. Quantitative work is clearly privileged in discussions of the application of chaos/complexity to any substantive area of science" (1998: 55). Byrne has noticed that not everyone realises this, and reports on the disappointment he felt when he thought he had spotted a proper complexity research programme: "despite the presence of the word 'complex' in the title, [the programme] seems to be proceeding in a way which is not connected with the implications of the chaos/complexity programme for quantitative social science. This is a very great pity" (Byrne, 1998: 122).

Apparently, not everyone believes that complexity research is quantitative in its very nature. Non-mathematical approaches to complexity often reflect a disbelief that "complex" refers to an external condition. With Chia, quite a few complexity scientists believe that "complex" is a qualification that emerges from the relationship between the researcher and researched. Stewart and Cohen, for example, write that complexity "is a property of a description of an object, not a property of the object itself" (1997: 67). Rosen, too, contends that "a system is complex if we can describe it in a variety of different ways, each of which corresponds to a distinct subsystem. Complexity then ceases to be an intrinsic property of a system, but it is rather a function of the number of ways in which we can interact with the system and the number of separate descriptions required to describe these interactions. Therefore, a system is simple to the extent that a single description suffices to account for our interactions with the system; it is complex to the extent that this fails to be true" (Rosen in Mikulecky, 1995). On a different level, Cilliers (1998: 2-4) argues that the difference between simple and complex is not an absolute difference but often a function of the observer's *distance* to the phenomenon being studied: "a little aquarium can be quite simple as a decoration (seen from afar), but as a system it can be quite complex (seen from close by)". In all of these cases, complexity is no longer accepted as a quality of the system itself, and some authors even suggest that "complexity is in the eye of the beholder" (Senesac, 1995). Thus, in contrast to what Chia asserts, complexity science does not necessarily presume that 'complexity' or 'the complex' is simply out there. In fact, some authors go as far as to suggest that the study of complex systems should receive special interest exactly *because* it acknowledges the importance of the engaging subject. "In comparing how the frameworks construct the relationship of knower to known, [Malisky and Holditch-Davis] suggest that whereas positivism posits the knower and known as independent from one another, and naturalism sees knower and known as inseparable and interactive, complexity sees them inseparable, interactive and moreover able through their interactions to create an emergent third system that would encompass both knower and known" (Hayles, 1999a).

*Reflexivity, Interactions ...*

According to Chia, the science of complexity should be understood, first and foremost, as a science that is based on a Platonic world view, one in which "essences" collectively constitute "fixed and unchanging realms of reality". Chia's counteroffer to the science of complexity, which he terms "complex thinking", starts with the premise that the world does *not* come to us as already "discrete and unchangeable". The stabilised world, he argues, is but the effect of the "taxonomic orientation" of the modern Western man: "the world is presented to us as naturally differentiated and hence isolatable and locatable into pre-existing systems of classification" (Chia, 1998: 346-9). According to Chia, being the scientists that they are, complexity scientists fail to remember that the clearly identifiable and well-demarcated objects of science are only clearly identifiable and well-demarcated because they have *made* them that way. But while many complexity scientists do indeed not question the realness of their fixed research objects, others do.

Chia believes that the taxonomic urge inevitably kills that which it frames. By "arresting, stabilizing and simplifying [what] would otherwise be the irreducibly dynamic and complex character of lived experience", complexity scientists are left with nothing but "solid inert objects". Therefore, and contrary to those who seek to address the "fluid living nature", complexity scientists deal with dead material only (Chia, 1998: 346, 362). Cilliers denies that complexity scientists have committed themselves to studying the inanimate. He contends that the research object of the complexity scientist, the complex system, is *inherently dynamic*: "in order to constitute a complex system, [its] elements have to interact, and this interaction must be dynamic" (Cilliers, 1998: 3). James agrees that complexity scientists are

60

necessarily in the business of studying dynamics and fluidity: "a complex system is not a complicated arrangement of material elements. It is a complex set of inter-relationships between elements which have attributes. Alteration of one sub-set of relationships alters the relations between all the elements. The relations between the elements define the system" (1999). According to these authors, studying complexity is all about addressing dynamic relationships. Lissack and Roos rephrase that message in the language of popular management books. According to them, complexity scientists are primarily concerned with "the arrows, not the boxes" (1999: 2).

*Reflexivity, Interactions, Time ...*

Quoting French philosopher Henri Bergson, Chia (1998: 349) contends that complexity scientists study "a world that has no history" and are therefore "condemned to deal with 'a world that dies and is reborn at every instant'". But an author like De Landa turns to complexity science exactly *because* it helps him put things in a historical perspective. He claims that in "a very real sense, reality is a *single matter-energy* undergoing phase transitions of various kinds, with each new layer of accumulated 'stuff' simply enriching the reservoir of nonlinear dynamics and nonlinear combinatorics available for the generation of novel structures and processes. Rocks and winds, germs and words, are all different manifestations of this dynamic material reality, or, in other words, they all represent the different ways in which this single matter-energy *expresses itself*". He believes that "structures as different as sedimentary rock, animal species, and social classes may be viewed as historical products of the same structure-generating processes" (1997: 21, 215; original italics). The kind of research De Landa engages in is very different from that which is carried out under the Grand Complexity Project. While complexity scholars of the latter kind arrive at their mathematically formalised accounts of reality by cutting away all references to time and place, De Landa tries to make sense of 'real life' manifestations of matter-energy by studying the spatio-temporal circumstances of their emergence. Cilliers follows De Landa in his stressing the importance of history. In classical mechanics, he argues, "time was reversible, and therefore not part of the equation". In the case of complex systems, however, this presumption of the reversibility of time no longer holds: "not only do [complex systems] evolve through time, but their past is also co-responsible for their present behaviour ... Any analysis of a complex system that ignores the dimension of time is incomplete, or at most a synchronic snapshot of a diachronic process" (Cilliers, 1998: 4-8). Juarrero, too, writes that complexity research is necessarily a form of historical research. She writes that "far from representing messy, noisy complications that can be safely ignored, time and context are ... central to the identity and behavior" and concludes that "complex systems are essentially historical. They embody in their very structures the conditions under which they were created" (Juarrero, 1999: 8). Judged by these authors' readiness to accept the importance of the effects of time, there is little reason to support Chia's claim that as a natural science, complexity science "is able to deal only with isolatable and instantaneous presents, where the past is not inextricably bound up with the present" (1998: 349).

*Reflexivity, Interactions, Time, Nonlinearity …*

According to Chia, "the very idea of a 'science' of complexity paradoxically entails the systematic reduction or simplification of otherwise vague and indefinable complexes of sensations into a taxonomic language that lends itself to quantifiable measures and to purposeful action". As a form of scientific analysis, complexity science is therefore all "about the development of an instrumentalized form of thinking primarily concerned with the construction of tools for aiding our adaptive actions" (1998: 345-6). In other words, according to Chia complexity scientists use complexity science to render the world something that they can manage at will. In reality, many complexity ideas and concepts are anything *but* instrumental to purposeful action. Take nonlinearity for instance, a key concept within the complexity discourse. Meiss (2000) defines nonlinearity as follows: "nonlinear is defined as the negation of linear. This means that the result f may be out of proportion to the input x or y. The result may be more than linear … or less than linear … Thus the fundamental simplifying tools of linear analysis are no longer available " (Meiss, 2000; italics added). Nonlinearity "guarantees that small causes can have large results, and vice versa", and thus makes it difficult if not impossible to predict how a complex system will react to a certain input (Cilliers, 1998: 4). Moreover, since the behaviour of a complex system is the outcome (function) of *ongoing* interactions between its elements, what is an input at some point in time soon becomes part of the output which, on its turn, is the input for the next interactions to take place, and so on and so forth; nonlinearity thus reinforces the unpredictability of its own effects.

Closely related to this issue is Chia's claim that the programme of modern Western science is one of exclusion. If a phenomenon does not lend itself to "algorithmic compressibility", i.e. if it does not lend itself to "the principles of operationalism", it is automatically deemed "non-existent". Chia believes that the complexity scientist, like any other scientist, is incapable of dealing with anything that withstands being compressed into an isolatable object: "all analysis is thus a translation into the pre-defined symbols of representation and the organizing codes associated with them" (Chia, 1998: 345, 358). Chia understands scientific analysis as a form of *Gaze*. "The Gaze is penetrating, piercing, fixing, objectifying. It is a violent act of forcibly and permanently 'present-ing' that which otherwise would be a fluxing, moving reality". Opposite of the Gaze, where "focus is achieved at the expense of the exclusion of the context", Chia places the *Glance*. The Glance accepts "the primacy of the unfocused" and refuses *not* to see that which the

62

scientific method excludes from attention. The Glance allows for the invisible to be seen, the unspeakable to spoken, and the unaddressable to addressed (Chia, 1996: 361-5). This is where the phenomenon of nonlinearity becomes important again. According to Cilliers, nonlinearity guarantees that when we model the world (which is necessary if we want to have some understanding of it) and certain things get left out (which is a logical consequence of simplifying act of modelling) we have no way of knowing the significance of what is *not* taken into account: "in a non-linear world where we cannot track a clear causal chain, something that may appear to be unimportant now, may turn out to be vitally important later. Or *vice versa*, of course" (Cilliers, 2001; original italics). Their acknowledgement of the phenomenon of nonlinearity forces complexity scientists to take an interest in seemingly trivial events or insignificant processes. And contrary to what Chia claims is true, some complexity scientists *do* believe that a raised interest in 'details' may have been invoked by something as fuzzy as "intuition". Coffman (1997), on this matter, suggests that complexity science, as a paradigm, teaches us to recognise the significance of "weak signals", situations in which "something just 'feels funny' about the behavior of a particular system. There's something different happening and we can't quite pin it down". For Coffman, complexity science is interesting precisely because it compels us to pay attention to that which is "new", "surprising", and "difficult to track down".

*Reflexivity, Interactions, Time, Nonlinearity, Self-Organisation & Emergence ...*

Another important concept from the complexity vocabulary is *self-organisation*. Like the notion of nonlinearity – we do not know how the system will respond to what we 'feed it' since result f may be out of proportion to input x – the concept of self-organisation undermines Chia's claim that complexity science is best understood as an attempt to "technologize" the world. In this process, "the world is first *broken up* into clear-cut, definite things occupying clear-cut, definite places in space and time, and in so doing creating a freely available pool of infinitely usable resources which can be combined and recombined in an infinite number of ways. These differentiated elements can then be reconstituted as a temporary 'assemblage' to meet immediate functional needs" (Chia, 1998: 347-8; original italics). The counterargument to this 'managerial' understanding of complexity science is that when a complexity scientist acknowledges the ability of a complex system to organise *itself*, he or she basically admits that there are very real limits to what outsiders can do for or to the system: "self-organization is a process in which pattern at the global level of a system emerges solely from numerous interactions among the lower-level components of the system. Moreover, the rules specifying interactions among the system's components are executed using only local information, without reference to the global pattern. In short, *the pattern is an emergent property of the system, rather than a property imposed on the system by an external ordering influence*" (Camazine et. al, 2001; italics added). This definition

63

makes clear that self-organisation is closely related to "emergence", a concept that also plays a vitally important role in complexity science.

While Chia sees complexity theory as part and parcel of modern Western science, Juarrero (1999: 21) maintains that complexity scientists' recognition of 'emergent properties' hacks into one of the very foundations of that modern Western science, namely that wholes are no different from aggregates, i.e. from agglomerations the properties of which remain the same whether or not they are components of a larger unity. A complex system has "emergent properties", meaning that as its elements interact in a nonlinear fashion, the history-laden complex system self-organises towards a state where a "renewed repertoire of behavioral alternatives and properties" can suddenly become available to it (Juarrero, 1999: 142-3). Emergent properties cause the whole to be more than sum of its parts. Analytical dissection so as to find out what accounts for this 'gap' is useless since the "aggregate activity" of the complex system is "not derivable from the summations of the activity of individual components". An emergent quality, in other words, "is roughly a quality which belongs to a complex as a whole and not to its parts" (Joslyn and Rocha, 2000; Broad, 1925: 23).

Concepts like self-organisation or emergence can hardly be seen as supportive of an attempt to "technologize" the world. In fact, one could go as far as to say that these notions are the ultimate arguments *against* the idea that the world can be brought under an external regime of control.

## PROBLEMS WITH THE WAR ON FADDISM (CONTINUED)

The main conclusion that can be drawn from the review of Chia's critique of the science of complexity is that there is no such thing as *the* science of complexity in the first place, and that it makes more sense to assume that there are *sciences* of complexity or different theories of complexity *within* the science of complexity. The fact that these theories are not rarely incompatible with one another has important implications for the research programme Maguire and McKelvey have in mind. As argued above, these authors believe that before complexity scientists can start exchanging research findings, it is necessary that they first reach consensus on how to integrate and synthesize all the ideas and concepts they bring together from diverse disciplines. Maguire and McKelvey insist that absent this consensus, attempts to apply complexity to management will not be founded on firm foundations, which will leave them vulnerable to faddism. Maguire and McKelvey justify this claim by arguing that their comprehensive set of instructions for rigorous research incorporates lessons from the past: "the record is clear over the past several decades – management ideas that do not become legitimised by resting on a foundation of quality research are quickly replaced by the next fad coming

down the pike" (1999: 19). I have strong doubts about the clarity of this record.
I believe there is no evidence whatsoever to support the claim that only quality
research as defined by Maguire and McKelvey can save complexity. In fact, I believe
that if any record *is* clear, it is that successful application of new ideas *never* rested
on Maguire and McKelvey's foundation of quality research.

In the following I will critically review Maguire and McKelvey's recipe against
faddism by retrospectively applying it to the introduction of other 'alien sciences'.
I will first claim that there is no historical evidence that students of organisation
have ever waited for consensus in the exporting field before they started applying
alien ideas and concepts to organisation. After that, I will argue that there is very
little to support Maguire and McKelvey's claim that nothing good can come from
eclecticism. Lastly, and this will be done in relatively great detail, I will try to show
that students of organisation have neglected what Maguire and McKelvey call "the
tough work of rigorous definition and operationalization", but that their 'loose'
approach to matters has not stopped these students of organisations from still
benefiting from the ideas and concepts they borrowed.

## No Consensus

Maguire and McKelvey have found that in the "young and nascent field" of
complexity science, "a unified view or theory has not yet been built" (1999: 24).
From their choice of words it can be concluded that the authors foresee – or hope, at
least – that a solid, full-grown and internally consistent theory of complexity will
be available at some point. I do not share Maguire and McKelvey's positive outlook
on this matter for already within a *single* discipline, scholars seem unable to get
their act together and develop a widely agreed upon theory.

Take warfare studies, for instance. It is widely accepted that this field of research
has been an important source of inspiration for students of organisation (see e.g.
Levy, Alvesson and Willmott, 1999). Today we think that organisations, like
armies, should have 'strategies'. It is also not uncommon for those involved in
(the study of) organisations to talk about 'lines of command', about 'tactics', about
'divisions', or about 'conquering' and 'defending' a market. The source from which
these and many other ideas and concepts were borrowed is or has ever been a
"unified view or theory" (see De Landa, 1991). Still, nothing indicates that the
absence of "a consensus on how to integrate and synthesize all the ideas and
concepts these students of warfare bring together", to paraphrase Maguire and
McKelvey, has stopped students of organisation from applying these ideas and
concepts to organisation. They have not waited for warfare scientists to reach an
agreement on what e.g. "strategy" really is, and have "charged ahead with the
building of models [and] entire organization theories and management
philosophies" on "corporate strategy". And quite successfully so.

65

## No All-or-Nothing

Based on the assumption that consensus *is* within reach and that a unified theory of complexity *will* be available at some point, Maguire and McKelvey insist that students of organisation should not embrace this theory half-heartedly: as a student of organisation, you either work with complexity theory or you don't. And if you do, you do not merely use those concepts you like, "based on whatever is convenient or has a nice metaphorical ring to it". Maguire and McKelvey consider an opportunistic or eclectic treatment of the science of complexity useless because complexity is a serious science with an equally serious research programme that only works if you pay respect to its internal consistency. But the record on this matter is again far from clear. Evidence to support the claim only an 'all-or-nothing' strategy towards new ideas and concepts can stave off faddism is hard to find. It appears that when students of organisation turned to warfare studies, to stay with the previous example, they were quite fussy about what ideas and concepts they actually wanted to use. While a fair number of ideas and concepts *have* been imported to the realm of organisation, many other *have not*. In other words, even if we accept for the sake of the argument that there is such a thing as *the* science of warfare, it is clear that students of organisation did not swallow it whole. Especially in the light of Maguire and McKelvey's insistence that concepts need to be defined and operationalised rigorously (discussed hereafter), in many cases – genocide, raping and pillaging, firing-squads – we should be grateful that students of organisation *have* been selective in their appreciation of what the warfare discourse has to offer. What is perhaps more relevant for this particular discussion, the fact that many ideas and concepts were not imported does not seem to have hampered the 'success' of a concept like strategy in the world of organisation. Apparently, successful application of alien concepts does not depend on the co-introduction of all other related ideas and concepts.

## No Rigour

The third claim Maguire and McKelvey make is that faddism is inevitable unless we commit ourselves to "the tough work of rigorous definition and operationalization" (1999: 23-5). This claim is fully consistent with how they see the relationship between organisation and complexity science. Maguire and McKelvey believe that deep down, in their very essence, organisations *are* complex systems. This means that the concepts we use to describe complex systems are the very same concepts we use to describe 'the particular complex systems that are organisations'. Within this view it therefore makes perfect sense to maintain that when we apply concepts like emergence, nonlinearity, strange attractors or fitness landscapes to organisation, we do *not* use those words metaphorically. When used correctly, these ideas and concepts refer to the reality of organisation. If, on the other hand, we do not use these concepts correctly, i.e. if we (inadvertently) engage in "oversimplification" or "superficial treatment", these concepts lose all value. I see no compelling reason to accept this scenario. I don't believe that "loose application" necessarily leads to meaningless concepts. There is nothing that indicates that students of organisation have taken great interest in the 'core meaning' of the concepts they borrowed, let alone in applying them rigorously. In fact, I believe that if alien ideas and concepts have *not* gone faddish in the field of organisation, it is often *because* these ideas and concepts have not been defined and operationalised rigorously. It is my conviction that only 'tailor-made' ideas and concepts – ideas and concepts that have been reshaped to fit their new habitat – appear to stand a good chance of surviving in the realm of organisation. The process that describes the tweaking of new ideas and concepts, the fiddling with them so as to make them fit their new home is perhaps best illustrated in the discussions on the role metaphor plays in scientific inquiry.

## Metaphors Gone Literal

The claim that there is more to complexity than mere metaphor bears testimony to a distinct philosophical position in which metaphorical descriptions are categorically separated from descriptions that represent a phenomenon *as is*, i.e., from literal descriptions. According to this line of reason, you either grab your subject matter by its essence, in which case 'you tell it like it is', or you discuss it in an inapplicable language, which makes you either a poet or a liar. Other philosophical positions lead to different appreciations of metaphor, however.

Gareth Morgan (1980, 1983, 1986) thinks of metaphor as a lense and argues that with every other metaphor we 'look through', we disclose more and more of the same organisation. Others have radicalised Morgan's conclusion that the difference between literal and metaphorical is problematic and claim that a fundamental difference between the two simply does not exist (see e.g. Letiche and Van Uden, 1998). These authors deny that the world is already 'out there', that language has the capacity to describe that world in a neutral, unbiased fashion, and that we, as "re-searchers" or "dis-coverers" are thus in the business of finding the particular language that "re-presents" that world accurately. Instead, language is said to 'produce what it denotes'. This argument will be discussed in somewhat greater detail in chapter 5, but for now it suffices to say that according to these authors, organisation is not a given object that awaits our correct description of it. This has far-reaching consequences for how metaphor is valued. Instead of accepting an ontological distinction between right (literal) and wrong (metaphorical) descriptions, it is now assumed that *if* there is a line that separates between different kinds of descriptions, it is the line that separates standard, old, embedded, ingrained, normal descriptions on the one hand from new, speculative, surprising, odd ones on the other. As Nietzsche (1872: 50-1) describes the situation, "the only intrinsic difference here is the difference between custom and novelty, frequency and rarity". If the difference between metaphorical and literal is a difference of degree rather than of kind, it means that one can only discriminate between normal and novel understandings of organisation. To illustrate this point, I will show that the 'career' of the concept of organisational culture was one in which metaphors slowly became literal descriptions. The underlying process I will then apply to complexity, arguing that the success of complexity will ultimately be determined by the extent to which complexity ideas and concepts contribute to existing organisational research programmes.

*The Culture Example*

The concept of organisational culture is a relatively novel one. In 1985 Edgar Schein writes that "the fields of organizational psychology and sociology have developed a variety of useful concepts for understanding individual behaviour in organizations and the ways in which organizations structure themselves. But the dynamic of why and how they grow, change, sometimes fail, and – perhaps most important of all – do things that don't seem to make any sense continues to eludes us". Here is where Schein inserts culture: "the concept of organisational culture holds promise for illuminating this difficult area. I will try to show that a deeper understanding of cultural issues in organizations is necessary not only to decipher what goes on in them but, even more important, to identify what may be priority issues for leaders and leadership". According to Shafritz and Ott (1992: 481-3), the organisational culture school essentially accused the dominant research groups of that time of "using the wrong tools (or 'lenses') to look at the organizational elements to understand and predict organizational behavior" and proposed new, tentative, weird concepts to describe organisational life. However, less than two decades later these once-odd concepts are part of the 'official' language of organisations and today a satisfactory answer to the question "could you tell me about the culture of your organisation?" is as real and valid a description of that organisation as is the answer to a question like "could you tell me about the structure of your organisation?". Slowly but surely the speculative, 'inappropriate' concept of culture has become a concept that we believe says something meaningful about organisations.

One of the consequences of culture becoming part of normal organisational discourse was that the concept more or less liberated itself from its roots. That is, in the course of time the ties between the 'original' meaning of culture and its meaning in the field of organisation loosened, allowing organisational culture to become an 'autonomous' concept – an *organisational* concept in its own right. This is an important phenomenon, and especially so against a background in which Maguire and McKelvey stress the need for "rigorous definition and operationalization".

Initially, when organisational culture was still an underdeveloped concept, its theorisation depended heavily on the literature that inspired the organisational culture school in the first place. Schein aimed to "provide a clear, workable definition of organizational culture that takes into account the accumulated insights of anthropologists, sociologists, and psychologists" (1985). Armed with the insights of these anthropologists, sociologists and psychologists, students of organisation then faced the challenge of importing the notion of culture and its sub-concepts (heroes, sagas, rituals, artifacts, norms, dominant values, etcetera) to the field of organisation in a way that made sense. What if these students of organisation would have committed themselves to Maguire and McKelvey's guidelines for serious research? Let us presume that at some point all anthropologists, sociologists, and psychologists reached overall consensus on what culture is. Even in this feigned situation, it is not clear why students of organisation would be interested in a widely agreed upon definition of culture. What is important for them is that the concept of culture 'works' in the realm of organisation. Above all, this requires that concepts like culture, heroes, sagas, rituals, artifacts or norms bear relevance to the *existing organisational discourse.* Schein got interested in culture because he believed a deep understanding of the workings of culture may help identify priority issues for leaders. The value of the concept of culture to this student of organisation was thus determined by the extent to which this concept contributed to an existing research programme on leadership. In general, for the introduction of an alien concept in the field of organisation to make sense, that concept needs to 'earn its place' in existing organisational research projects. The concept of culture needs to be capable of being used to say something useful about dysfunctional bureaucracies, for example, or it must add something to our understanding of inter-departmental communication, or feed the discussion of the meaning of computers in a work environment, or contribute to the debate why people are hesitant to share their information with colleagues, and so on.

When the concept of culture was inserted into existing discussions of organisation, the link between the meaning of culture in an organisational context and its 'original' meaning began to weaken. In accordance with how anthropologists, sociologists and psychologists used the concept, Schein still saw culture as a "conceptual tool" to describe things and processes. The author thus understood the concept of culture as *descriptive* in its intent: organisational culture "can illuminate individual psychological behavior; what goes on in small groups and in geographically or occupationally based communities; how large organizations work; and how societal, multinational issues can be better understood through increased cultural insight. A dynamic model of culture will be especially useful in improving our understanding of how human systems evolve over time" (Schein, 1995). Shafritz and Ott also believe that a firm understanding of the culture of an organisation helps us better understand the nature of that organisation. In particular, it makes us aware of the limits of rational approaches to organisational affairs. "A strong organizational culture literally controls organizational behavior: for example, an organizational culture can block an organization from making changes that are needed to adapt to a changing environment. From the organizational culture perspective, the personal preferences of organizational members are not restrained by systems of formal rules, authority, and by norms of rational behavior. Instead, they are controlled by cultural norms, values, beliefs and assumptions. In order to understand or predict how an organization will behave under varying circumstances, one must know and understand the organization's patterns of basic assumptions – its organizational culture" (1992: 482). Here, as was the case for Schein, organisational culture is a concept that is still of the same 'nature' as *normal* culture: a concept that helps identify and describe the inherent features of some form of social life, in this case organisational life. But Paul Jeffcutt shows that in the course of time, the meaning of the concept of organisational culture diversified. Jeffcutt argues that "a number of contradictory discourses have become constructed and embellished in order to give coherence to the differing positions in the interpretation of organizational culture". One of those discourses he describes as "culture as a corporate (managerial) possession, (aka 'Corporate Culture)". This "managementcentric" reinterpretation of organisational culture has had important consequences, Jeffcutt believes. "A remarkable turnaround or critical inversion appears to have taken place [in organisation studies] in which the manipulation of the non-rational has become the latest tool of managerial control, i.e. organisations have been rendered predictable and controllable (and thus 'rational') through the management of the irrational (culture). Thus rather than 'bounded rationality' we now have 'bounded irrationality', functioning to harmonise, integrate and unify organisation" (Jeffcutt, 1993: 25-6; 1989: 23). In describing the effects of organisational culture falling into the hands of 'management thinkers', Jeffcutt points at a phenomenon that is very relevant for our discussion: was culture initially defined as a lense that helps us see the limiting reality of the nature of organisations, in the course of time it *also* came to be understood as a sophisticated management tool with which formerly uncontrollable organisational dynamics can be brought under control.

Jeffcutt's example summarises at least two important and closely related aspects of the practice of applying alien ideas and concepts to organisation. First, a concept will acquire multiple and sometimes even mutually exclusive interpretations sooner or later. Second, concepts become increasingly independent of their 'root meaning'. As time went by and the concept of culture nestled itself in its new habitat, *organisational* culture slowly came to be considered a phenomenon in its own right. As a result, and this can be concluded from the literature references they make, students of organisational culture lost interest in the original writings by anthropologists, sociologists and psychologists and turned to books and articles that were already about *organisational* culture. Over the years the meaning of the concept of organisational culture thus emancipated itself from the meaning of 'normal' culture. The case of culture is not unique in this respect. Above I already argued that for one reason or the other, students of organisation thought it made sense to borrow the concept of strategy from the warfare sciences. In the field of organisation studies, strategy, like culture, came to be interpreted in many different ways. And in the very same way that students of organisational culture 'got the idea' at some point and stopped reading books written by anthropologists, students of *organisational* strategy eventually could no longer be bothered to keep track of new theories of strategy developed back in the field of warfare studies. Consequently, the military associations of the concept of strategy faded out, and business strategy became an organisational phenomenon in its own right.

The process that Maguire and McKelvey (1999: 25) refer to as the "importing and translating" of ideas and concepts can be summarised as follows. On an ongoing basis, students of organisation go shopping for ideas and concepts in other disciplines: they read into alien discourses, select the ideas and concepts they like, and disregard the unappealing ones. These students then try to fit the newly adopted ideas and concepts into their existing organisational research programmes. While some imported ideas and concepts are rarely used and die out, others 'make it' and become part of normal organisational discourse. What successfully introduced ideas and concepts have in common is that they gradually lost their association with the source from which they were derived and became proper *organisational* ideas and concepts.

## COMPLEXITY AND ORGANISATION

I do not expect students of organisation to approach the science of complexity in a way that is fundamentally different from how they welcomed e.g. culture studies. That is, in the same way that these students have applied the concept of culture to organisation to get a better understanding of "individual behaviour in the context of organisation" or "the way organisations structure themselves", ideas and concepts from the complexity discourse will be appreciated for how they connect with existing discussions on organisational themes. Maguire and McKelvey themselves actually seem to support this view. In their eyes, the New Science is well on its way toward short-lived faddism unless serious research shows that "CEO's using the New Science produce more competitively advanced firms than CEO's who do not" (1999: 57). Maguire and McKelvey's norm for successful "importing and translating" is clearly not of an 'intra-complexity science' nature, but is instead defined in very specific managerial terms: does complexity science help us build competitively advanced firms or does it not? Other students of organisation value complexity for very different reasons. Letiche (2000: 555), for example, hopes to find that complexity theory can "provide us with ethnographies of emergent action" while Irvin uses insights from the science of chaos and complexity to scrutinize "one of the main features of the conventional credo of organizational management: the 'ethic of self-preservation'" (2002: 359). Svyantek and Brown have reasons to believe that the representation methods associated with complex adaptive systems studies, and in particular its theories of the way in which agents interact with each other so as to form coherent, self-reinforcing clusters, may be useful in developing a better understanding of the US automobile industry (2001: 42-3). And having first pointed out that theories of complexity have already been used in studies on "organizational transformation", on "corporate strategy", and on "organization design", Styhre, Ingelgard and Roth set out to examine "the notion of knowledge from the non-linear, nonreductionistic perspective put forth by complexity theory" (2000: 51).

My attempt to apply complexity to organisation is thus but one of many. And my project too is part of a more comprehensive research programme. I do not turn to complexity science because I am convinced organisations really *are* complex systems. As such, I do not believe that rigorous application of the complexity discourse grants me direct access to the very being of organisation. I do not believe the discourse of organisation can be replaced with the alleged 'deeper' discourse of complexity and that organisations can therefore be safely stripped of all that makes them look like proper organisations – which is precisely what one does if one proposes to abstract departments, meetings or managers into "stochastically idiosyncratic agents". In this study, the ideas and concepts of the science of complexity are appreciated for their (potential) contribution to the development of the idea that organisations are living entities. This not only means that only those complexity concepts will be explored that appear relevant in the light of that project, it also implies that I have no intention to be truthful to the core meaning of complexity concepts and apply them rigorously. Still, from my 'confession' that I will take an opportunistic approach to the science of complexity, it should not be concluded that I believe that complexity science has no 'intrinsic' value to it – far from it.

The reason why students of organisation resort to the use of ideas, words or even entire models developed in other disciplines is because they expect that these ideas, words and models have something to add to existing research projects. An alien concept is deemed valuable because it offers something that was not already available to the student of organisation. There are many ways in which a new concept can make a valuable contribution to existing research. A new concept may enable us to see and describe a phenomenon that was invisible or inexpressible in our pre-existing language, for instance. Alternatively, we may borrow a concept to undermine the foundation of a dominant theory we seek to destroy. Or we hope to find that the alien concept combines existing organisational themes in a way that was inconceivable in the absence of it. In any of these cases, the concept must connect to an existing research project, but, and this is an important but, it should not be fully consumed by the latter. The 'value added' of the concepts we borrow is that they make a difference, one way or the other. Put differently, given that we turn to the use of new concepts *because* they add something to an existing discussion, it makes no sense to kill its potential by sterilising it – by arguing, for example, that the concept we borrow from complexity science is really but a synonym for an already existing organisational concept. The successful import and translation of alien concepts boils down to a balancing act: for the concept to be relevant, it needs to fit into existing research programmes. At the same time, if we want to preserve the potential we appreciated the concept for in the first place, we must be careful not to let the concept be fully assimilated into and taken over by that which we already know.

What I hope to find in this study is that ideas and concepts from the sciences of complexity bear relevance to the project of theorising organisational aliveness – the idea that organisations live lives of their own. In the following three chapters I will try to find out in what way and to what extent that is actually the case.

# 3

# Organisational Aliveness: a Systems Perspective

## INTRODUCTION

In the first chapter I discussed the main changes that took place at Vitesse after Karel Aalbers was appointed president. Based on how the New Vitesse presented itself, I constructed the Official Vitesse Story – the formal report on the transformation of a football club into a "multi-entertainment football company". According to this story the Vitesse Way was prompted by a recognition that Vitesse was not all that it could be and that today's Vitesse needed to become the Vitesse of Tomorrow, described in the company's mission statement. In the eyes of Aalbers, the gap between today's Vitesse and the ideal Vitesse can only be closed if he and his followers take a fresh approach to matters: 'things' need to be organised in a radically different way. In the Official Vitesse Story, Aalbers plays a key role in the process of professionalisation: it was Karel Aalbers who acknowledged Vitesse's great potential, it was Aalbers who saw what needed to be done to actualise that potential, it was Aalbers who designed and built the organisation to make it happen, and it is Aalbers who now supervises the correct handling of the Vitesse organisation. I argued that a close reading of the Official report on the process of 'reinventing Vitesse' reveals the distinct image of organisation that shines through it. To describe the Official understanding of the Vitesse organisation and the link between Aalbers and that organisation in particular, I drew an analogy based on my understanding of the relationships between a sculpturer, an imagined work of art, the raw material, and the instruments the sculpturer uses: Aalbers (the sculpturer) sees what today's Vitesse (the raw material) could very well be: the Vitesse of Tomorrow (the imagined work of art). After having assured himself and others that the transformation is possible, Aalbers then determines the kind of organisation (instrument) he believes he needs to convert Vitesse as it stands today into the

Vitesse of Tomorrow. What is characteristic of the thus constructed *organisation-as-tool* view is its presumption that the organisation exists for someone and something other than itself: the Vitesse organisation comes after and is therefore a derivative of Aalbers' plans to realise the Vitesse mission statement. I showed that when Aalbers was forced to resign as president of Vitesse, his explanation was fully consistent with this instrumental understanding of the Vitesse organisation: Nuon stole the Vitesse organisation from Aalbers, and only so to use it for Nuon's *own* purposes. In the organisation-as-tool view, the organisation remains inanimate an object that functions the way its owner wants it to function. As argued, in this study I will try and develop an alternative for this view, namely a complexity science-informed approach to organisations that allows the latter to be thought of as living entities.

In this chapter I will focus on the work of complexity scientists who argue that complexity theory is really complex *systems* theory and that as such it is closely related to 'normal' systems theory. I will first discuss what this normal systems theory came to look like when it was applied to organisation, after which I will show what changes when we go from understanding organisations as tools to seeing them as (complex) systems. I will then argue that systems theory and thinking of organisations as living entities go very well together because understood as systems, organisations *themselves* interact with their environments. In this chapter I will try to theorise organisational aliveness through the concept of organisational learning. Chapter 3 ends with a brief discussion of whether or not complex systems theory amounts to more than sexed up normal systems theory.

## Systems Thinking in Organisation Theory

In chapter 2 reference was made to an attempt to "develop a common explanatory framework to talk about animals, machines, and humans" (Hayles, 2000: 246). Cybernetics, the interdisciplinary research programme that emerged from that enterprise, was well-received by students of organisation. Shafritz and Ott (1992: 263) believe that in the late 1960s organisation theory was simply ready for everything cybernetics stood for. "The human relations orientation had lost much of its vigor, and the cultural milieu was moving away from the introspective, self-developmental optimism of the 'flower-child generation' and the 'T-groups' of the early 1960s. Society was becoming enamored with computers, statistics, heuristic models and information systems". Two closely related developments spurred the 'paradigm change' in organisation theory: the application of Ludwig von Bertalanffy's general systems theory and the use of quantitative tools and techniques to understand the complex relationships between organisational and environmental variables.

systematic . xxx    (cyber)

Complex SYSTEMS theory.

systemic. ✓✓✓

The general systems view is based on the assumption that *any* organised collection of parts united by prescribed interactions and designed for the realisation of goals can be a system. When an organisation is understood as a system, one "views an organization as a complex set of dynamically intertwined and interconnected elements, including its inputs, processes, outputs, feedback loops, and the environment in which it operates and with which it continuously interacts. A change in any element of the system causes changes in other elements ... systems theorists see organizations as always-changing processes of interactions among organizational and environmental elements. Organizations are not static, but rather are in constantly shifting states of dynamic equilibrium. They are adaptive systems that are integral parts of their environment. Organizations must adjust to changes in their environment if they are to survive; in turn, virtually all of their decisions and actions affect their environment". Systems thinking came with a quantitative research programme. Sharing with Norbert Wiener that "cybernetics is mathematics or it is nothing", organisation theorists showed "an extensive reliance on quantitative analytical methods and models" by applying "mathematical and statistical probability models to organizational processes and decision making" (Shafritz and Ott, 1992: 263-5).

Reed writes that the "core conceptualization of an organization as a purposive social system geared to the fulfilment of a relatively stable set of environmentally induced needs for security, integration, continuity and survival has formed the theoretical bedrock of the systems framework in organizational analysis. Around this core a veritable plethora of auxiliary concepts and theoretical innovations have been woven with the aim of making systems analysis more dynamic – that is, better equipped to explain the causes and consequences of organizational change. This has encouraged the analytical shift towards an 'open systems' view of the organization" (Reed, 1992: 80).

In 1966, Daniel Katz and Robert Kahn argue that "because organisations are open systems, they must continuously adapt to changing environmental factors, and managers must recognize that all organizational decisions and actions in turn influence their environments" (in Shafritz and Ott, 1992: 266). The authors argue that the open systems approach "begins by identifying and mapping the repeated cycles of input, transformation, output, and renewed input which comprise the organizational pattern. This approach to organizations represents the adaption of work in biology and in the physical sciences by Von Bertalanffy and others. Organizations as a special class of open systems have properties of their own but they share other properties in common with all open systems. These include the importation of energy from the environment, the through-put or transformations of the imported energy into some product form which is characteristic of the system, the exporting of that product into the environment, and the reenergizing of the system from sources in the environment. Open systems also share the characteristics of negative entropy, feedback, homeostasis, differentiation, and equifinality. The law of negative entropy states that systems survive and maintain their characteristic internal order only so long as they import from the environment more energy than they expend in the process of transformation and exportation. The feedback principle has to do with information input, which is a special kind of energic importation, a kind of signal to the system about environmental conditions and about the functioning of the system in relation to its environment. The feedback of such information enables the system to correct for its own malfunctioning or changes in the environment, and thus to maintain a steady state or homeostasis. This is a dynamic rather than a static balance, however. Open systems are not at rest but tend toward differentiation and elaboration, both because of subsystem dynamics and because of the relationship between growth and survival" (Katz and Kahn, 1966). According to Reed, the most influential sub-stream within the open systems framework was so-called contingency theory. This theory "concentrates on the immediate pressures that organizations face in their task environments and internal structural accommodations which they have to make to meet these challenges. Factors such as volatile market demand, technological change and political realignments within the environment are identified as key 'contingencies' which organizations have to respond to in the appropriate manner if they are to ensure their long-term survival ... Environmental change is seen to create new sources of uncertainty for the organization in that the course of future developments is unpredictable and the appropriate response required from the organization to meet the challenge posed by these changed circumstances becomes problematic" (Reed, 1992: 80-1). Shafritz and Ott argue that contingency theory is a "close cousin" of systems theories, one "in which the effectiveness of an organizational action (for example, a decision) is viewed as dependent upon the relationship between the element in question and all other aspects of the system – at the particular moment. Everything is situational: there are no absolutes or universals" (Shafritz and Ott, 1992: 267).

What are the main consequences of imposing the systems framework on the phenomenon we are interested in here? The single most important observation pertains to the very 'ontological quality' of organisation. The organisation-as-tool school as developed in chapter 1 essentially sees the organisation as a means to an end – a necessary evil almost, something the master is forced to work with if he wants to reach the goals he set for himself. When we switch to the systems view, the organisation moves to the foreground. By discussing and theorising the survivability of organisations, system theorists seem to argue that the organisation *itself* matters. What is more, by claiming that organisations are capable of performing activities like "adapting", "facing" or "achieving", systems theorists appear to think of organisations, not as passive instruments, but rather as phenomena that can 'do things' themselves, as living entities. Systems theory and thinking of organisations as living entities apparently go together very well.

*autopoesis*

Gareth Morgan even goes as far as to suggest that one follows logically from the other: "let's think about organizations as if they were organisms. We find ourselves thinking about living systems" (1986: 39). In this chapter I will go deeper into this partnership between organisational aliveness and the systems framework.

## FROM TOOLS TO SYSTEMS

Given that this study seeks to develop the notion of organisational aliveness in contradistinction to an instrumental take on organisation, it makes sense to explore the main differences between the systems perspective and the organisation-as-tool view that follows from the Official Vitesse Story.

The Official understanding of the Vitesse organisation rests on three closely related assumptions. The first assumption is that there can be no organisation without an organiser. The Official Vitesse Story insists that success is made from blood, sweat and tears, meaning that it was only because Aalbers took action to change Vitesse's hopeless situation for the better that the club still exists today. A squad that is capable of posing a serious threat to 'the top', the fervid yet inoffensive social atmosphere in the Gelredome, the feeling of belonging to a family – everything is there because Aalbers organised for it. In addition to being responsible for designing and building it, Karel Aalbers is also Officially required to look after it. The Vitesse organisation not only needs a creator, in other words, it also needs someone to keep it functioning. The second assumption that underlies the Official understanding of the Vitesse organisation is that an organiser organises for a reason. This reason *comes before* and is *external to* the Vitesse organisation. What justifies the very existence of the Vitesse organisation is the set of objectives that Aalbers wanted to realise. Thus, far from being self-referential, the organisation exists by the grace of its *functionality*. The third assumption that underlies the Official understanding of the Vitesse organisation follows almost automatically from the previous two: an organisation always and only reflects the deliberate goal-driven decisions of the organiser. Put differently, the organisation is nothing but the 'materialised' answer to the question of exactly how the organiser thinks he is going to realise the goals he has in mind. The concept of structure helps to illustrate this point.

A very common way for a company to communicate 'how things are organised' is through a (visual) representation of its *structure*. Unilever, for instance, presents its company structure as follows: "Unilever's organisation is designed to be effective. Dedicated to the needs of the future, our structure clarifies roles, responsibilities and decision making so that we can deliver outstanding performance across our business". Structure, in other words, images the purposeful arrangement of things at a given point in time. Studying Unilever's structure tells you for example that the "Executive Committee is responsible for agreeing priorities and allocating resources, setting overall corporate targets, agreeing and monitoring business group strategies and plans, identifying and exploiting opportunities created by Unilever's scale and scope, managing external relations at the corporate level and developing future leaders", or that "the regional presidents are responsible for delivering business results in their respective regions. Regional presidents report to either the director of the Foods division or the director of the Home and Personal Care division. As members of either the Unilever Bestfoods or Home and Personal Care divisions, they play an important role in shaping divisional strategy and ensuring that regional strategies and plans are consistent with overall objectives" (see Unilever website). A structure shows that everything is 'there' and 'so' for a reason. Like Unilever, or any other self-respecting organisation for that matter, Vitesse has a corporate structure. Vitesse's organisation chart[8] offers a schematic overview of what the Vitesse management team thinks are the issues that need to be organised for. In chapter 1 it was shown that the overall mission statement consisted of different sub-missions, such as wanting to be a championship candidate, wanting to be part of the fans' daily lives, wanting to be a decent employer and so on. Vitesse's company structure shows that these sub-missions consist of yet smaller 'sub-sub-missions' that all need to be organised for. Wanting to win the title, for instance, requires that Vitesse organises for high-quality medical attention for its players and that the club maintains a sound scouting apparatus. The company structure thus reveals what Vitesse has decided are the sub-activities that need to be carried out in the light of the overall mission statement. The corporate structure also discloses what Vitesse apparently thought was the best way to cluster these sub-activities into departments. For instance, one learns that activities like running a kids club, maintaining press relations, and publishing Vitesse media are all considered forms of *communication*, and that these activities can therefore be grouped into a communications department. Lastly, the organisation chart tells us about the decisions that were made regarding the question of who should be in charge of the various departments (this person here, that person there, ...) and to whom these heads of these departments must report (managers to the CEO, the CEO to the president, ...). In short, the organisation chart captures in a snapshot the answers to questions of exactly how things are to be dealt with – of how the organiser believes one should organise for success.

At least on the face of it, to understand the organisation of Vitesse as a complex system is to call into question these three assumptions of the organisation-as-tool view.

## Introducing Complexity

As said, an instrumental understanding of organisations assumes the necessity of someone doing the actual organising. This changes when we accept the complex systems perspective. Stewart and Cohen, for instance, argue that "to some, organisation implies the existence of an organiser, as the existence of a watch implies that of a watchmaker. This is a seductive line of argument, but there is no compelling reason to accept it. One of the most remarkable features of organic matter – and, we now realise, inorganic matter too under suitable circumstances – is its ability to organise *itself*". These authors therefore believe it is very well possible to conceive of "an organised structure that comes into being without conscious intervention" (Stewart and Cohen, 1997: 14; original italics). The phenomenon of self-organisation also undermines the Official presumption of functionality – the idea that organisations are always there for some external reason. Paul Cilliers maintains that "since the self-organising process is not guided or determined by specific goals, it is often difficult to talk about the *function* of such a system. As soon as we introduce the notion of the function, we run the risk either of anthromorphising, or of introducing an external reason for the structure of the system" (1998: 92; original italics). The Official understanding of structure is also disputed when we start to think of organisations as complex systems. The organisation-as-tool view offers Aalbers as the originator of the Vitesse organisation, as the person who thought it up and built it. This enabled the Official Vitesse Story to present the structure of the Vitesse organisation as a reflection of Aalbers' determining that 'this is what the organisation will look like'. Complex systems thinking leads to a very different conclusion: "the structure of the system is not the result of an *a priori* design", Cilliers writes (1998: 91; original italics). But if structure does not mirror the decisions of the external designer (because there need not be one) and if structure does not result from functionality (because complex systems are not necessarily goal-directed), what, then, *does* explain the structure of a complex system? According to Cilliers, the keyword, again, is self-organisation: "internal structure can evolve without the intervention of an external designer or the presence of some centralised form of internal control. If the capacities of the system satisfy a number of constraints, it can develop a distributed form of internal structure through a process of self-organisation" (Cilliers, 1998: 89).

From this brief introduction to complexity alone it can be concluded that the central role Aalbers plays in the Official Vitesse Story will not be maintained if we take an organisation-as-complex-system view. Understood as a complex system, the Vitesse organisation no longer depends on Aalbers to formulate the goals that give the organisation a reason to be. Moreover, the Vitesse organisation no longer needs Aalbers to design its internal structure. In fact, the Vitesse organisation qua complex system no longer depends on Aalbers to do the organising: it can organise itself. But if Aalbers is no longer the very *conditio sine qua non* of the Vitesse organisation, what is the relationship between Aalbers and the organisation of Vitesse?

## From Master to Element

The Official Vitesse Story positions Aalbers *outside* the Vitesse organisation or, to be more precise, *on top of it*. Aalbers is a visionary, someone who not only has already seen the 'Vitesse that Could Be' but who also knows what kind of organisation it takes to build that Vitesse of Tomorrow. Furthermore, to the extent that Aalbers does not have the time or the skills to deal with details, Aalbers can take the information generated by his management-specialists and integrate it into his overall understanding of the situation. Either way, Aalbers grasps the situation in its totality – he sees the big picture. Understood as a complex system, however, there is no vantage point from which Aalbers oversees the area. Applying complexity theory to organisation, Streatfield argues, means that "the perspective immediately shifts from that of an objective observer of an organization ... to that of a participant in the living present of a local situation" (Streatfield, 2001: 129-30). Cilliers too points out that complexity thinking leads us away from the idea of an all-knowing designer and towards an image in which the components of a system live on local knowledge only. "Each element in the system is ignorant of the behaviour of the system as a whole, it responds only to information that is available to it locally. This point is vitally important. If each element 'knew' what was happening to the system as a whole, all of the complexity would have to be present *in that element*. This would either entail a physical impossibility in the sense that a single element does not have the necessary capacity, or constitute a metaphysical move in the sense that 'consciousness' of the whole is contained in one particular unit" (1998: 91-4, 5; original italics). If we apply this line of argument to Vitesse, Aalbers is no longer capable of taking a helicopter-view on matters; now there is only so much information he can collect about his Vitesse organisation.

In the Official Vitesse Story, the president's comprehensive understanding of the overall situation at Vitesse enabled him to change the Vitesse organisation as he thought was right. When we understand the Vitesse organisation as a complex system, however, there is not only so much that Aalbers can *know*, there are also serious limitations to what the Vitesse president can *do*. The one-on-one correspondence between Aalbers' actions and the effects these actions have on the Vitesse organisation is missing. First there is non-linearity. As argued in chapter 1, the phenomenon of non-linearity guarantees that small causes can have large results and vice versa. The word 'can' is carefully chosen here. Non-linearity does not guarantee that small causes *will* have large effects – they might, but we simply don't know. The notion of non-linearity forces us to admit that the effects of actions are very difficult to predict, and especially so in the long run. The interactions that define the complex system 'cross-interact', they reinforce and temper one another, push each other in different directions, merge into patterns which interact with other elements and patterns, and so on. As a result, what the Vitesse organisation 'is' and 'does' is not for Aalbers to decide. "What we have is a self-organising process in which meaning is generated through a dynamic process, and not through the passive reflection of an autonomous agent that can make 'anything go'", Cilliers writes (1998: 116). The move towards the organisation-as-complex-system perspective thus implies that Aalbers, in addition to being no longer omniscient, stops being capable of fully mastering the Vitesse organisation, changing it as he thinks is right. As Cilliers phrases it: "single elements cannot contain the complexity of the whole system and can therefore neither control nor comprehend it fully" (1998: 122). If Aalbers is but one of the many system elements that matter, if he has limited knowledge of his organisation only, and if the effects of his actions are unpredictable, what can still be said about his contribution to the overall functioning of the Vitesse organisation? Here the concept of *weight* becomes important.

In his discussion of neural networks and its relevance for our understanding of the functioning of the brain, Cilliers argues that "any single neuron receives inputs from, and provides input to, many others. Complex patterns of neural excitation seem to be the basic feature of brain activity. A simple mathematical model of a neuron can be constructed. A neural unit uses the sum of its inputs to decide what output to generate. Each input is, however, first multiplied with a certain value or 'weight'. This weight determines the connection strength between two units, and models the characteristics of the synapses in the nervous system. The output response of any specific neuron (let us call it A) is therefore calculated in the following way: the outputs of all the neurons connected to A are – after having been multiplied in each case by the weight associated with the connection between that specific neuron and A – added together. This sum is multiplied with A's transfer function to generate A's output. This output becomes one of the inputs to the next neuron in the network, after it has in turn been adjusted by the value of the weight in that pathway. The value of the weight can be positive or negative. The transfer function is (in all but the most trivial cases) a non-linear function. Neurons form part of the large networks with complex connection patterns, and since the weights determine the influence of one neuron on another, the characteristics of a network are mainly determined by the values of these weights". By stressing the importance of the weights that determine the connection between nodes in a network, Cilliers offers an alternative to the analyses of those who hold that meaning is stored in the nodes *themselves*. "In a full-blown neural network no node has any specific significance. As explained earlier, the significance lies in the values of the *weights*; not, and this is crucial, in the value of any specific weight or even group weights, but in the way they are related and activated each time" (Cilliers, 1998: 27, 33; original italics). If we apply this line of reason to the Vitesse

*network analysis*

organisation it follows that Aalbers *by himself* is of no special importance. While this does not imply that Aalbers stops being significant altogether, it does mean that the influence Aalbers has on the functioning of the Vitesse organisation is far more difficult to estimate than it was under the organisation-as-tool view. If the Vitesse organisation is a complex system, Aalbers' importance to that system cannot be determined in absolute terms or even understood as function of how 'well-connected' he is. His importance is derived from and distributed among "patterns of weight values in the whole system" instead (Cilliers, 1998: 28).

In the picture that emerges from the analysis above, the relationship between Aalbers and the Vitesse organisation is understood very differently from how the Official Vitesse Story sees it. At a very basic level it can be concluded that the move towards systems thinking implies that Aalbers' position changes from being *on top of* the Vitesse organisation to being *part of* it, and that the relationship between the Vitesse organisation and Aalbers seems to have changed from one of 'tool to master' to one of 'system to element'. The disappearance of the external controller leaves us with the question of what accounts for a system's continuing existence. In the absence of someone to look after it, why does a system not cease to be? Below, without going into any 'details', I will show how systems thinkers theorise a system's capacity to maintain itself and why, for example in the case of Vitesse, the (coming and) going of system elements does not seem to affect the system as a whole.

## Perpetuating Patterns: How Systems Maintain Themselves

Systems theorists propose the following line of thought: elements interact and from these interactions a system emerges. This system maintains itself as 'the system' by regenerating the elements it consists of. The circular character of this process has been termed *autopoiesis*, a pseudo-Ancient Greek word for self-creation or self-production. Maturana and Varela (1987) originally defined autopoietic systems as follows: "an autopoietic system is organized (defined as a unity) as a network of processes of production (synthesis and destruction) of components such that these components (i) continuously regenerate and realize the network that produces them and (ii) constitute the system as a distinguishable unity in the domain in which they exist". In a slightly different way, Zeleny describes an autopoietic system as "a system that is generated through a closed organisation of production processes such that the same organisation of processes is regenerated through the interaction of its own products (components), and a boundary emerges as a result of the same constitutive processes" (in Khalil and Boulding 1996: 123). Autopoietic systems thus engage in a process of 'self-constitution through self-reference' (see Blom, 1997: 22).

What is characteristic of autopoietic systems is that it is not so much the material make-up that defines their being as it is the *pattern* that emerges from the

84

interactions between system elements. Kauffman (1995: 20-1) uses the term "dynamic order" here, and illustrates this phenomenon by discussing the Great Red Spot. "The Great Red Spot vortex [on the planet Jupiter], essentially a storm system, has been present for at least several centuries. Thus the lifetime of the Great Red Spot is far longer than the average time any single gas molecule has lingered within it. It is a stable organization of matter and energy through which both matter and energy flow". Dynamic order, the phenomenon that living systems (have to) change to stay the same, does not just take place in outer space. Kauffman sees an "intriguing similarity" between the Great Red Spot and the human organism, "whose molecular constituents change many times during a life" (Kauffman, 1995: 20-1). Hayles[9] shows that Kauffman's understanding of the human being is very similar to Norbert Wiener's, who "suggests that human beings are not so much bone and blood, nerve and synapse, as they are patterns of organization. He points out that over the course of a lifetime the cells comprising a human being change many times over. Identity cannot therefore consist in physical continuity". In Wiener's own words: "we are but whirlpools in a river of ever-flowing water. We are not stuff that abides, but patterns that perpetuate themselves" (Hayles, 1999: 104; Wiener, 1954: 96).   HERACLITEAN.

*[margin notes: excellent. pleas for a physical ache. Scotland.]*

But what does it mean for a system to perpetuate itself? As argued earlier, central to systems thinking is the system-environment differentiation. Accordingly, a system that maintains itself as a distinguishable entity is a system that manages to uphold this differentiation – it keeps the environment out, so to speak. From this it should not be concluded that a system is somehow independent of its environment: a system needs to interact with its environment because pure self-reference or direct circularity is sterile, informationally empty. Self-referentially closed systems need to interrupt their self-referentiality, they need to 'open' themselves to the outside and allow information to enter. As Luhmann phrases it, "if [the system] were not continually irritated, stimulated, disturbed and faced with changes in the environment, it would after a short time terminate its own operations, cease its autopoiesis" (Blom, 1997: 27; Luhmann quoted in Blom, 1997: 26). It is important to stress that while a system's capacity to maintain itself depends on informational penetration by the environment, the environment does not *determine* the behaviour of the system: an environment cannot have a causal influence on a self-referentially closed system without the cooperation of the system itself, as Luhmann formulates it (in Blom, 1997: 26). A self-referential system is self-referential exactly because its actions are internally motivated. Based on their study of the 'visual system' of frogs, Maturana and Varela see "the activity of the nervous system as determined by the nervous system itself, and not by the external world; thus the external world would only have a triggering role in the release of internally-determined activity of the nervous system" (quoted in Hayles, 2000: 139). "The difference between an event 'triggering' an action and 'causing' it may seem to be a quibble, but for Maturana the distinction is crucial. Causality implies that information moves across the boundary separating an organism from its environment and that it makes something happen on the other side. Say you slap me and I become angry. In the conventional view, one would say that your slap caused me to be angry. As this inference indicated, a causal viewpoint organizes the world into subject and object, mover and moved, sender and receiver. The world of causality is also the world of domination and control. Maturana sought to undo this perception by positing that living systems are operationally closed with respect to information. A system acts always and only in accord with its organization. Thus events can trigger actions but they cannot cause them because the nature and form of a system's actions are self-determined by its organization" (Hayles, 2000: 141).

If we apply these systems dynamics to the phenomenon we are interested in here, it follows that as a complex system, organisation can no longer be thought of as a lifeless object: the behaviour of a complex system is neither determined by an external organiser, nor is it directly caused by its environment. If systems do not slavishly reflect the instructions of *others*, then we are getting close to thinking of organisations as living *lives of their own*. But what does it mean for an organisation to be imagined 'alive' in the first place?

## A LIFE OF ITS OWN

Recall the discussion on the career of the concept of organisation culture. In chapter 2 I indicated there is no reason to believe that culture is intrinsic to organisation. That is to say, there is nothing that suggests that organisations always had cultures in them, that we happened to notice these cultures at some point, and that researchers then set out to accurately describe them – merely representing what was already there. The reality of organisational culture, I would argue, is best understood as the effect of successful attempts to *attribute* 'features of culture' to organisation. For one reason or the other, some students of organisation became interested in cultural studies, borrowed ideas and concepts that anthropologists normally use, and applied them to organisation. Apparently, and again for one reason or the other, the concept of culture fell on fertile ground. In the course of time, it became increasingly normal to suggest that like societies at large, organisations have cultures. Today, the reality of what was once an awkward, speculative concept simply seems taken for granted: there *is* such a thing as organisational culture. The very same line of argument applies to the phenomenon of 'organisational aliveness'. I do not believe one could ever prove that organisations live lives of their own. Organisational culture came to be regarded as real because people slowly began to accept that features of culture (rituals, heroes, artefacts, values, myths) apply to organisation just the same. Similarly, organisations will be said to live lives of their own if we manage to successfully attribute 'indicators of aliveness' to organisation.

Systems theorists have already 'equipped' organisations with a number of characteristics that we ordinarily think of as typical of living entities: the organisations-as-system is assumed to be *aware* of its own existence, for example, and *understands* that in order to *maintain itself*, it needs to *survive*. The organisation is not only believed to be *sensitive* to the signals it receives from its environment, but is also said to be capable of *interpreting* them. An environment does not determine the behaviour of a system. Instead, the organisation actively *responds* to the inputs it receives, and so on. In the following I will focus on another possible indicator of organisational aliveness, namely an organisation's ability to *learn*.

## The Official Vitesse Story or Why The Past Doesn't Matter

Learning implies that the past matters. Below I will first show that the Official Vitesse Story, in its appraisal of the relevance of the future, downplays the significance of the past. I will develop the complexity science-informed argument that the past, far from being over, plays a vital role in the behaviour of organisations.

To understand what role 'the past' plays in the Official Vitesse Story it is helpful to first say something about what *kind* of story the Official Vitesse Story is. The Official Vitesse Story is perhaps best understood as an epic, as defined by organisation theorist Paul Jeffcutt. He describes an epic as "a perilous journey" that contains a struggle and, in the end, "the exultation of the hero". An organisational epic is usually structured as follows: "a typical ordeal would begin with the identification of an organization's attachment to traditional working practices that were outmoded but unchallenged ... Redemption occurs through the heroic struggle with these limitations (such as radical structuring, transformations in employee and managerial effectiveness), and culminates in the organization's assertive rebirth and the subsequent burgeoning". The author goes on to argue that "with vision, charisma and belief identified as the special qualities that enable the successful attainment of this quest" epics of this kind are usually concerned with "the mystical properties of leadership". With regards to how the story achieves its effect, Jeffcutt points out that an epic is a very imposing form of narrative. "The narrator here typically adopts the position of one who has witnessed the attainment of the quest, and hence uses the voice of a prophet or evangelist in dispensing persuasive strategies to encourage others". Jeffcutt therefore concludes that epics, as representational strategies, are characterised by "heroic quests for closure" meaning that they "expose an overriding search for unity and harmony that suppresses division and disharmony. In this project these texts express overwhelmingly monologic voices that seek to achieve authority and persuasion through the suppression and proscription of dialogue" (Jeffcutt, 1993: 29-32).

The Official Vitesse Story is a straightforward and unnegotiable presentation of the triumphal march of its president. After having first established the overall miserableness of the early 1980s – references to the deplorable state of Vitesse in the pre-Aalbers period are part of the "club folklore", Van Mierlo writes (2001: 30) – the Official Vitesse Story introduces local hero Karel Aalbers who accepts the challenge of saving Vitesse, and commences a difficult journey in which he averts all sorts of dangers and solves a variety of seemingly insolvable problems. What is characteristic of epics is that the hero, in a very real sense, puts the past behind him: a slain dragon no longer poses a threat and a swamp needs not be crossed twice. In Arnhem, we have seen, the past consists of things such as bad results on the pitch, financial deficits, very few fans, overall cynicism, and poor facilities. The Vitesse epic stresses these 'issues' have all been dealt with successfully– they are problems overcome. The Official representation of the Gelredome helps to illustrate this point. The new stadium is "a vision realised", the much battled-over but inevitable answer to the inaptness of the old Nieuw Monnikenhuize stadium. But given that the 'housing problem' was but one of many issues, there is no time for complacency. "In my opinion, after years of saving money we finally have that Formula 1 car. Now that we have it, we've got to face the responsibility of driving it, of making it happen" (Aalbers in *Haagsche Courant*, 7 November 1998). One problem has been solved, but a new challenge already awaits. "A light has dawned, a certain superiority has come to Vitesse. The Gelredome can lend a hand in this process but cannot go it alone. For the Vitesse management team, the subject of Gelredome is closed. It is there, in all its splendour. Henceforth, the issue of the 'top club-feeling' will be on the top of the agenda ... the Monnikenhuize feeling was great, but now we have to go on" (Rood in Vitesse, 1998: 87). In short, in the Official Vitesse Story only the *future* matters. Aalbers makes decisions that he believes will help transform today's Vitesse into the envisioned Vitesse of Tomorrow. The Vitesse organisation, understood as a reflection of Aalbers' wilful decisions, is therefore future-driven.

In the following sections, by linking the development of the Vitesse organisation to the notion of learning, I aim to show that the past *did* matter to Vitesse. Before I will argue that organisations *themselves* are capable of learning, I will first review the argument that, in the end, it is always *the individuals inside the organisation* who do the learning.

### Individual Memories or Why The Past Matters

In spite of the Official claim that Aalbers' position was unquestioned, not everyone praised the Vitesse president to the skies. In chapter 4 I will show that non-official Vitesse stories make clear that various (groups of) individuals held some form of grudge against the Vitesse president: overruled managers, external parties whose deals with Vitesse Aalbers undid, sponsors who felt betrayed as the Vitesse president moved on to more promising prospects, close business friends who found out that Aalbers' friendship seemed financially motivated, belittled members of Vitesse's supervisory board, and so on. As far as Aalbers was concerned, the 'issues' these parties had could be largely ignored for they were part of the past and thus inconsequential to the future-driven Vitesse organisation. Others come to a very different conclusion with regards to the relevance of the past.

Van Mierlo points out that Aalbers repeatedly trumpeted his low esteem of the Vitesse supervisory board. According to Aalbers there was not much for the members of the supervisory board to do, other than to sit and nod as the club president carried out his plans. Not surprisingly, the members of the supervisory board were not all too happy with how Aalbers spoke of them. In the eyes of Aalbers, however, their feelings were of no significance since it was already decided that there would be no room for the current members of the Vitesse supervisory board in the future anyway. But Aalbers was wrong to think that the supervisory board's 'attempt to thwart the process of building the Vitesse of Tomorrow' would soon fall into the category of problems that Aalbers fixed over the years. In chapter 4 I will show that Aalbers' spending frenzy left Vitesse on the edge of immediate bankruptcy and that shirt sponsor Nuon was only willing to lend Vitesse money if the club relieved itself of its president. Van Mierlo believes this is the moment when Aalbers' disdain for the members of the supervisory board backfired on him: the board was more than willing to meet Nuon's demands. Van Mierlo goes as far as to conclude that it was not so much the great debts Vitesse was in that brought an end to the era of Karel the Emperor as it was the "unbearable" behaviour of Aalbers (Van Mierlo, 2001: 22, 48).

When we understand learning in a conventional way, demonstrating the importance of individual memories in organisations is quite easy: president shows little respect to members of supervisory board, members of supervisory board keep this maltreatment in mind, members take revenge on president when opportunity comes along. The case for *organisational* memory, which also presumes the importance of the past, is far more difficult to make.

## Organisational Memories or Why The Past Matters

Systems, we have seen, maintain themselves by dealing with the inputs they receive from their environments. "Which are the possible coping mechanisms open to a system faced with changing external conditions? Two extreme positions can be identified. At the one extreme, the structure of the system is fully defined *a priori*. This would mean that the system is 'hard-wired', and that all possible eventualities will have to be catered for in the fixed, internal structure of the system. Apart from the loss of adaptivity, such systems may become too cumbersome in complex situations. Under less complex conditions, 'hard-wired' systems, operating on simple control principles, may be an adequate solution, but this is not a plausible option for the kind of complex system we are interested in. At the other extreme we may have systems with no independent internal structure at all, but where the structure is fully determined by the conditions of the environment. A system which merely mimics the environment directly will not be capable of acting in that environment since it will be fully at its mercy. To be able to interpret its environment, the system must have at least the following two attributes: some form of resistence to change, and some mechanism for comparing different conditions in order to determine whether there has been enough change to warrant some response. Both these attributes merely translate into the need for a form of memory – without resistence to change, memory is impossible. If the self-organising capabilities of such a system are adequate, it will then *learn* to cope with a changing environment" (Cilliers, 1998: 99; original italics). How is one to conceive of systemic (organisational) learning and memory?

One is perhaps inclined to think that the fact that the (main) constituents of an organisation are human beings who are all capable of learning themselves bears relevance to the organisation's capacity to learn, and that organisational memory can be inferred directly from the individual memories of the people within that organisation. However, if we think of organisations as complex systems, then this kind of extrapolation does not work. Garfinkel describes the 'explanatory leap' from part to whole as follows. "In classical reductionism, the behaviour of holistic entities must ultimately be explained by reference to the nature of their constituents, because those entities 'are just' collections of the lower-level objects with their interactions. Although it may be true in some sense that systems 'are just' collections of their elements, it does not follow that we can *explain* the system's behaviour by reference to its parts, together with a theory of their connections. In particular, in dealing with systems of large numbers of similar components, we must make recourse to holistic concepts that refer to the behaviour of the system as a whole" (Garfinkel, 1987: 202-3; original italics). The general conclusion that the behaviour of complex systems cannot be explained by looking at the behaviour of its constituents very much applies to the phenomenon of systemic learning.

An important finding in complexity research is that the 'intelligent' behaviour of a system does not require that the constituents of the system are intelligent also. This becomes apparent in e.g. Edelman's study of the workings of the brain. His research shows it is not the elements (or their inherent capacities) themselves that matter but rather the connections and interactions between them. Edelman (1987) argues that the brain is capable of performing "higher functions", in spite of the fact that the brain consists of a large population of simple, undifferentiated yet interconnected neurons only. These neurons are dynamically organised, meaning that the relationships between them are not fixed; they constantly change because brain reorganises itself on the basis of its interactions with the environment.

Cilliers summarises Edelman's model of the brain as follows: "the brain is pre-structured in a way that is general and non-specific, but with enough differentiation (i.e. enough asymmetry) to allow external influences a 'foothold'. The 'general' structure of the brain is then modified through experience and behaviour in order to reflect the specific circumstances encountered in the history of the system in question. The brain thus organises itself so as to cope with its environment" (Cilliers, 1998: 102-3).

In the foregoing discussion on how the past affects the present, the concept of memory was said to apply to individuals only: members of the supervisory board store information about their unpleasant encounters with the Vitesse president in the back of their minds and call this information into memory to inform their decision when they are asked to fire Aalbers. The model of systemic memory as developed by Edelman works in a rather different way. When a system interacts with its environment, the system *itself*, and not (just) its elements, preserves the information that is generated in these interactions. The Edelman model stresses these memories should not be thought of as discrete units of information that the system stores in specific locations. Information is instead "smeared" over the many units that constitute a complex system; the memory of a system is "stored in a distributed fashion" (Cilliers, 1998: 108, 95). This phenomenon relates to a complex system's capacity to reorganise itself. The system-environment interactions induce some "pattern of activity" within the system, i.e. they cause some nodes to relate to one another or modify existing connections between nodes. According to Edelman, if an environmental stimulus is a single event that does not occur again, the pattern it has brought about will "die out". However, if the event is significant, in the sense that it occurs more often, the pattern will be reinforced, causing the organisation of a system to be changed. Thus, even if the structure of a system initially reflects the design of an external agent, it will not continue to do so forever. "Internal structure can evolve without the intervention of an external designer or the presence of some centralised form of internal control. If the capacities of the system satisfy a number of constraints, it can develop a distributed form of internal structure through a process of self-organisation. This process is such that structure is neither a passive reflection of the outside, nor a result of active pre-programmed internal factors, but the result of a complex interaction between the environment, the present state of the system and the history of the system ... the system develops a stable structure that enables it to recognise important events through a process of self-organisation" (Cilliers, 1998: 89, 94). This model of systemic memory is radically different from a conventional understanding of learning that sees memories as distinct bits of information – data that an external apparatus is capable of storing, retrieving and processing. In the systems Cilliers and Edelman describe, learning takes the form of changes in the very being of the system. This phenomenon destroys the classical distinction between memories and that which processes those memories.

"Brains ... are constantly rebuilding themselves. As a result of such running modifications, the entire nervous system evolves as a whole, 'hardware' and 'software' alike, homing in on a structure that performs the required functions. The hardware/software distinction is thus irrelevant, if not downright misleading, and best forgotten. This means that there is no sensible way to distinguish systematically between building a nervous system, programming it, or providing it with data. A batch of sensory data comes in, changes the program, and the circuitry is rebuild accordingly. When the next batch of data comes in, it is received and processes by a *different* hardware system. This distinction cannot be emphasised too strongly" (Stewart and Cohen, 1997: 151; original italics).

At least when compared to a discussion of memory at the level of the individual, it seems that the notion of systemic memory as developed above allows for very few firm conclusions to be drawn. For example, if we want to explain Aalbers' involuntary resignation as Vitesse president through the concept of systemic memory, we would have to conceive of that event as an outcome of Vitesse reorganising its internal structure on the basis of its ongoing interactions with its environment. It is quite difficult to give some body to this abstract idea. The Edelman-based model of complex systems talks about collections of interconnected nodes. It is unclear exactly how this translates in realm of organisation. In the case of Vitesse, what or who are the equivalents of nodes? And given that the boundaries[10] that separate the system from its environment are anything but straightforward, which nodes do we include in our model and which ones do we disregard? If nodes are connected to each other, how and by what criteria are we to define the strengths of the connections? And what do changes in the connection strengths between the nodes look like in the case of the Vitesse organisation? The conceptual problems are enormous. Notwithstanding these practical problems, the very suggestion that organisations *themselves* could be capable of learning makes the concept of systemic memory important for this study.

In the Official Vitesse Story things are organised the way they are because Aalbers organised them that way. Understood as a complex system, on the other hand, the Vitesse organisation does not need a grand designer to amount to something; as a complex system, it can organise itself. Above, some introductory comments were made about the role a system's learning capacity plays in this process of self-organisation. It was argued that a system interacts with its environment, it reorganises itself by changing its internal structure. Here, contrary to what for instance Peter Senge (1990) writes about the learning organisation, the system does not depend on the learning capacities of the people inside the organisation. One could argue that the ability of an organisation to withdraw its own learning activities from those of its constituents 'demonstrates' its aliveness, i.e. that the organisation lives a life of its own.

Now that we have looked at some of the implications of moving from the organisation-as-tool view to understanding organisations as systems, it is time to explicitly address an important theme that has been pushed to the background thus far: the difference between 'normal' systems theory and complex systems theory.

## Normal Systems Thinking, Complex Systems Thinking

So far, our discussion has not discriminated between complex systems thinking and traditional open systems thinking. Some authors believe there is nothing that justifies such a distinction in the first place. Phelan (1999), for instance, writes that for "systems theorists, many of the central concepts in complexity theory are simply old wine in new bottles with an intellectual heritage that can be traced back to the pioneering work of von Bertalanffy, Ashby and Boulding". Mikulecky too finds that the question needs to be addressed whether or not "the self proclaimed 'revolution'" of the New Science really *is* a revolution and, again, not "merely old wine in new bottles" (2000). An example may help to show why many authors believe that complex systems theory does amount to more than mere repetition.

Shafritz and Ott show that early systems theorists already acknowledged that when elements of a system interact with one another, they hardly ever do so in a straightforward fashion: "the interconnections [between the elements] tend to be complex, dynamic, and often unknown; thus when management makes decisions involving one organizational element, unanticipated impacts usually occur throughout the organizational systems" (1992: 264). It seems that today's students of complex systems are better capable of addressing the 'wild' nature of the interactions between elements than were their predecessors. Part of the problem of normal systems theorists had to do with the foundation on which their theory was built. Early systems theory rested on the philosophy and methods of logical-positivism and was therefore strongly cause-and-effect oriented. Ott (1989) argues that system theorists eventually ran up against the inherent limitations of this framework and its particular view of the relationship between cause and effect: for every effect there must be an identifiable and proportional cause. Today's complexity theorists benefit from advancements within scientific inquiry. They are equipped with a firm understanding of non-linearity and are as such better capable of making sense of disproportional relationships between output (effect) and input (cause) than were 'old school' system theorists. Modern systems theorists see things early systems thinkers were incapable of noticing, they can map the world in ways that normal systems thinkers simply had no knowledge of, and they can explore phenomena with the help of techniques that were unknown to the first wave system thinker (see Meiss, 2000). Complex systems theory thus accepts the general concepts of normal systems theory but discusses them in a more sophisticated fashion. One could argue that by thoroughly revising it, complex systems thinking saves the open systems approach by making the latter 'sturdier', fuelling it with recent insights from the complexity sciences.

Quite a few authors maintain that complexity research does more than merely *explain* matters. They argue that knowledge about complex systems can also be *acted* upon.

## Better Organisations Through Complexity

Kauffman writes the following: "[the] wonderful possibility, to be held as a working hypothesis, bold but fragile, is that on many fronts, life evolves towards a regime that is poised between order and chaos. The evocative phrase that points to this working hypothesis is this: life exists at the edge of chaos. Borrowing a metaphor from physics, life may exist near a kind of phase transition. Water exists in three phases: solid ice, liquid water, and gaseous steam. It now begins to appear that similar ideas might apply to complex adaptive systems. For example, we will see that genomic networks that control development from zygote to adult can exist in three major regimes: a frozen ordered regime, a gaseous chaotic regime, and a kind of liquid regime located in the region between order and chaos. It is a lovely hypothesis with considerable supporting data, that genomic systems lie in the ordered regime near the transition to chaos. Were such systems too deeply into the frozen ordered regime, they would be too rigid to coordinate the complex sequences of genetic activities necessary for development. Were they too far in the gaseous chaotic regime, they would not be orderly enough. Networks in the regime near the edge of chaos – this compromise between order and surprise – appear best able to evolve as well" (Kauffman, 1995: 26). Many believe that hidden in Kauffman's biological jargon lie important lessons for students of organisation. Marion and Bacon (1999: 77), for example, explore the consequences of applying Kauffman's notion of 'robustness' to organisation. The authors argue that organisations possess a range of coupling patterns which "allow organizations to maintain relative stability in most environments and protect the system against severe shocks". Organisations must be stable enough to be able to absorb punches from the environment but only *relatively* so – they should not be rigid. Coleman comes to a similar conclusion. "The organization design/structure can facilitate change by being flexible. The concept is to design the organization for the purpose of evolution with the changing environment, to design for emergence by avoiding the rigidities of bureaucratic hierarchy. This means creating organizational arrangements that do not inhibit evolutionary change and that accept discontinuous change in the environment as entrepreneurial opportunity" (Coleman, 1999: 38).

94

Regine and Lewin (2000) narrow their exploration of the managerial value of complex systems thinking down a little and argue that the behaviour of complex adaptive systems teaches us a great deal about how companies are to be *led*. Regine and Lewin maintain that leaders "cannot afford to carry on with management methods that were developed in a different age and for a different type of business environment" and should adopt a "different mode of thinking". Like Wood (1999: 120), who also believes that "the principles of the new sciences ... can help leaders in both corporations and institutions of governance and policy making understand and address the challenge of change and adaption", Regine and Lewin believe that research on systems at the edge of chaos has shown that today's leaders are in the business, not just of leading, but of "leading at the edge". The authors "are seeing something fundamental in how to lead change in organizations so that it is more adaptable, and how to cultivate a culture in the workplace that is better able to embrace and create change". And they are not alone here. Regine and Lewin write that the "leaders we spoke to recognized that a mechanistic view of business had a very limited life in a global and connected economy, and that a holistic and biological approach was more appropriate for changing times. This perspective required an approach to an organization that was more organic". Leadership is not a matter of mastering the organisation – or no longer so anyway. Leaders should give up the "myth of control" and acknowledge that as complex adaptive systems, organisations *themselves* will try to adapt to changes in their environments. "Generally, in times of change flexibility is required. That means lots of experimentation to find what works and what doesn't, to discover new ways. In many of these organizations, the leaders had to do something differently in order to survive. The question they faced was how to change existing structures of the organization to provide greater capacity to adapt and to embrace change. None of the leaders had a design, but rather they proceeded blindly: relying on their intuition, guided by a consciousness that there had to be a better way of working, and armed with a few complexity principles. The workplace itself became an experiment in progress for them, which meant embracing the organization as an unfolding, unpredictable complex system. Not knowing where the experiment would lead them, the leaders made it explicit to their people that together they were embarking on an uncertain journey". Complex systems theory teaches us that proper leadership is something quite different from a boss who designs the organisational structure and then tells his workers what to do. It is the New Leader's task to facilitate self-organisation, creating the right conditions for it occur: "companies whose management is guided by principles of complexity science are organizationally flat, have fewer levels of hierarchy, and promote open and plentiful communication and diversity. Complexity science argues that these properties enhance a system's capacity for adaptability" (Regine and Lewin, 2000).

## Issues with Systems Thinking

In chapter 2 I argued at length that there is no such thing as 'the' science of complexity. What we are dealing with instead is a variety of 'schools', each of which understands and treats complexity in its own distinct way. In this chapter we have looked at the work of authors who believe that when you decide to do research on complexity, you end up studying the behaviour of complex systems. Complex systems thinking is commonly understood as advanced normal systems thinking. That is, complex systems theory accepts the basic framework of normal systems theory – the idea of a system that tries to survive in its environment – but theorises the dynamics of this process in a much more sophisticated way than 'old school' systems theory was capable of.

While large numbers of scholars see complexity theory as an extension of normal systems thinking, others are not convinced that complexity theory and systems thinking are compatible in the first place. Authors like Stacey or Streatfield, for example, feel that a full appreciation of 'the lessons from complexity' does not go very well with thinking of organisations as systems. Stacey finds the decoupling of complexity and systems theory necessary because, for one thing, systems thinking too often assumes the necessity of an external designer. "Most systems theories ... offer the prospect of control from outside the system, by a designer, and any transformation of the system must also be determined from outside by a designer" (Stacey, 2001: 70). And as Streatfield sees it, in your typical organisation-as-system view, "the movement of an organization into the future is the movement of a whole system from the present into the future. The essential function of management is to control that movement. To be 'in control', managers objectively observe the system. They analyze it rationally in order to design it and/or identify and act upon leverage points in such a way that movement into the future realizes or unfolds a future state already enfolded in the present/past. The future state is enfolded in the system in the form of its design and the implied archetypical patterns of that design, in the form of the potential action at leverage points, and in the form of vision formulated for it" (2001: 127). Unhappy with systems theory's alleged inherent presumption of the external designer, Streatfield and Stacey turn away from the notion of system altogether and propose to think of organisations as complex responsive processes instead. "From the perspective of complex responsive processes, an organization is not thought of as a system but, rather, as interconnected patterns of action in time and geographic space" (Streatfield, 2001: 129).

Whether or not Stacey and Streatfield are right to presume that the systems perspective is inextricably bound up with the notion of an external designer, their suggestion that applying complexity theory to organisation does not necessarily require a systems orientation remains important; apparently, not everyone believes that the 'classical' systems discourse, however refined, is suitable for discussing complexity. In the following two chapters the focus will be on the works of Stewart and Cohen. While this writers duo does not reject the systems approach as such (they *do* talk about systems), their contribution is deviant enough to justify studying it in greater detail. In chapter 4 I will take Stewart and Cohen's framework and use it to redefine the Vitesse organisation as an "emergent phenomenon". In chapter 5 I will show how I believe thinking organisations as emergent phenomena contributes to development of the idea that organisation live lives of their own.

4

# Rethinking the Vitesse Organisation

The purpose of this chapter is to introduce Stewart and Cohen, the authors whose ideas I will use to develop the notion of organisational aliveness in chapter 5. In this chapter I will apply Stewart and Cohen's model of emergent phenomena to Vitesse and show that this move leads to an understanding of the nature of the Vitesse organisation that is radically different from the one the Official Vitesse Story offers.

The application of Stewart and Cohen's framework requires that we pay attention to non-official Vitesse stories also – stories that make clear it is very difficult to uphold the Official claim that the Vitesse organisation is but the outcome of Karel Aalbers' intentional design.

## VITESSE AND NUON

When Aalbers is appointed president of Vitesse, he proves his reputation as 'seducer' by managing to talk various parties into investing in a football club that is as good as bankrupt[11]. The money Vitesse receives from the city of Arnhem, Akzo (now AkzoNobel) and various local companies saves the club from immediate bankruptcy and when Vitesse makes it to the *Eredivisie* in 1989, things really start to take off. Because of its good performance, both on the pitch and business-wise, Vitesse becomes less of a needy football club and more of an equal business partner. Aalbers is now in a position to deny its main sponsor *de Schoenenreus* the decision-making power this discount shoe retailer wants in return for its investment.
As far as Aalbers is concerned, Vitesse's autonomy is not for sale. Waste disposal company BFI becomes Vitesse's new shirt sponsor. The then newly appointed

director of BFI Paul Schaling explains that this sponsorship was completely unplanned for: "I invited Karel for a meeting. The purpose of that meeting was to inform Aalbers we wanted the money Vitesse owed us in two weeks. After an hour and half of talking, I had remitted a debt of € 136,000 and agreed to become Vitesse's main sponsor for an annual € 204,000. Even today, I still don't know how it happened". But Aalbers wants more, and the Vitesse president tries to bluff BFI into doubling the sponsoring fee. Aalbers tells Schaling that Delta Airlines wants to sponsor the club but that Vitesse wants to give BFI the opportunity to strengthen the existing relationship. BFI withdraws and Schaling congratulates Aalbers on his new found sponsor. The Delta Airlines-Vitesse deal does not come through, however, and at the beginning of the 1992/1993 season Vitesse has no shirt sponsor. That problem is solved when provincial governor Jan Terlouw introduces Vitesse to PGEM, a local energy company. According to Terlouw, a member of PGEM's supervisory board, sponsoring a football club will help the public utility communicate its new name, Nuon, to future clients. Name recognition among potential customers is important because the energy market is soon to be liberalised, which means that Nuon needs to catch the attention of customers who will be free to choose what company they want to buy gas and electricity from. Nuon president Tob Swelheim agrees to the proposal and his company becomes Vitesse's new sponsor.

## A Carefully Staged Coup

The relationship between Vitesse and Nuon appears to be a strategic partnership that enables both parties to become major players in their own field of business. According to the Official Vitesse Story, however, one of the so-called partners is up to something else: Nuon wants to take over Vitesse. A sports journalist summarises the coup as follows: "the energy trader lent Vitesse so much money that the club became fully dependent on its main sponsor. The well-remunerated [Vitesse] president was then dismissed and Nuon became the party in charge in the Gelredome. Nuon bought Vitesse for approximately € 27 million. That may seem like a lot of money but it is a real bargain. Nuon can use Vitesse to communicate with potential clients, both in the Netherlands and across borders. Any other energy supplier would be happy to spend much more to gain full control over a nice football club like Vitesse" (Van Nijnatten).

Henk Brouwer, Vitesse's treasurer until July 1999, says Vitesse came to depend on Nuon just before the official opening of the Gelredome stadium. Contractor BAM threatens to levy a distress on the Gelredome because Vitesse still owes BAM almost € 7 million. "After a full night and morning of negotiating a foundation was created. Vitesse had to put in € 4 million, Nuon the remaining 3 million. That immediately puts you in great debt" (in *De Gelderlander*, 2 December 2000). Nuon has very good reasons for wanting to participate in the Gelredome project. Vitesse and Gelredome are excellent marketing vehicles in that the Gelredome/Vitesse combination stands for everything Nuon wants to be associated with: innovation, ambition, demand-driven products, eagerness to conquer Europe, and so on. Nuon decides to 'help' Vitesse become a football club of stature. Without decent players, Vitesse will never make it to the European competitions, and without international success, Vitesse is simply not the kind of club Nuon wants to team up with. Therefore, or so the logic goes, it makes perfect sense for Nuon to see to it that Vitesse is able to afford fine players. Nuon is a substantial company and Swelheim encourages Aalbers to sign more and better players, thereby further increasing Vitesse's dependence on its sponsor. "Aalbers kept buying players. Nuon also demanded it, it wanted a good team. [Nuon] lent Vitesse almost € 11 million. Without that loan Vitesse would have already been bankrupt. We were up with our backs against the wall", as Brouwer describes the situation.

As Aalbers spends more money on players, expecting that Swelheim, as promised, will provide for the financial means, Nuon is looking for the right moment and the right way to carry out the coup. On 24 January 2000 Nuon invites Vitesse to present its financial situation to the members of Nuon's supervisory board. Nuon has always been aware of the great debts Vitesse is in but acts as if in shock. The sponsor offers to help: Nuon will lend Vitesse the money the club desperately needs, provided that the Vitesse supervisory board sacks Aalbers. If the board refuses to do so, Nuon will withdraw altogether and Vitesse will go bankrupt – a situation that the members of the Vitesse supervisory board will be held personally accountable for, as it was their legal duty to monitor Vitesse's financial situation. The Vitesse supervisory board complies with this threat and forces Aalbers to hand in his resignation, leaving Nuon with *de facto* full control over the Vitesse organisation.

Interestingly enough, Nuon itself never denied it was rather keen on the idea of taking over Vitesse. In France, public utility *Suez Lyonnaise des Eaux* had used the stable revenues from water and energy to build one of the biggest companies in the world of entertainment, Vivendi Universal. Vitesse fits Nuon's plans to do something similar. Nuon's director of communications Peter Knoers: "I came up with the idea of making Vitesse some sort of business unit [of Nuon]. The Netherlands are far behind other countries in that respect. In countries such as Spain, England and Germany it is not unusual for a club to fall into the hands of a company" (Van Mierlo, 2001: 65; Knoers in *De Gelderlander*, 24 February 2001). Aalbers had always opposed to such a scenario, however, and according to one of the interviewed Vitesse managers, Nuon was becoming very unhappy with the fact that while it was spending more and more money, it could not impose its will on Vitesse. "Nuon wanted to have a bigger say in terms of what happened at Vitesse. We even had a discussion on who was going to be the new head coach of Vitesse. No way. A sponsor does not mingle in discussions over who will be the new coach

... We said: 'thank you very much, you are a good sponsor. But the club determines the policy and you're the sponsor'". The interviewee makes Nuon a cynical compliment for the ingenious way it got its hands on Vitesse nonetheless. "We always said that Nuon would get ten percent of the Vitesse shares because of what it had done for us. Nuon now has forty percent. In my eyes they simply gave themselves a larger package of shares ... They would have never been able to pull that off with Aalbers still in place. Nuon knew that, Swelheim knew that ... Nuon got its shares for a much lower price than we would have agreed to. It is a real bargain for them: by getting rid of Aalbers, Nuon got itself a really good deal". At least initially, Nuon agrees to that latter conclusion. Swelheim argues that if anything, the acquisition of Vitesse is a token of sound entrepreneurship. In fact, to show that ownership of the Vitesse organisation is instrumental to the realisation of Nuon's *own* goals, Swelheim stresses he will not hesitate to sell Vitesse players if that serves the interests of Nuon best.

## Towards a Different Understanding of the Situation

The very idea that an organisation can be stolen, I argued in chapter 1, rests on the assumption that one can actually own an organisation. According to the Official Vitesse Story, Aalbers' ownership of the Vitesse organisation was guaranteed by the president's exclusive access to that organisation. Officially, Aalbers had every right to defend his monopolised control over the Vitesse organisation. Aalbers therefore needed to protect the Vitesse organisation against too much influence of his own management team, for instance. Given that "there can be only one captain" (Aalbers quoted by an interviewee), the Vitesse organisation would break adrift if Aalbers had to tolerate someone else in the cockpit. The members of Vitesse's supervisory board also pose a potential threat to the Aalbers' mastery over the Vitesse organisation. In the eyes of Aalbers, the very existence of a supervisory board carries within itself the danger of inhibiting the requisite manoeuvrability of the president. Supervision is deemed dysfunctional if it "stands in the way of adequate management". We have seen the Vitesse president keep sponsors at a distance also: as much as he appreciates financial contributions, Aalbers insists that a sponsor's money does not buy it influence over how the Vitesse organisation is run. The Vitesse fans, to give one more example, are denied direct access to the Vitesse organisation too. Club mottos like "people make Vitesse" or "Vitesse belongs to all of us" should not be misinterpreted as indicators of Aalbers' willingness to water down his control over the Vitesse organisation. What these slogans communicate instead is that Vitesse, as a company, has found an answer to the growing need of people to belong to some sort of community. References to the feeling of 'we are all in this together' and encouragements to act on that feeling merely reflect good entrepreneurship.

Below I will show that the Official claim that 'the Vitesse organisation answers to

Aalbers only' needs moderation. I will try to replace the crystal-clear image of "Aalbers runs Vitesse while Swelheim runs Nuon" with a much more turbid picture of intertwined interests, fading boundaries between professional and personal relationships and, ultimately, ambiguity in terms of who is running what. The purpose of the following section is to move away from the assumptions that underpin the organisation-as-tool view and make way for organisations to be understood as emergent phenomena.

## Aalbers and Swelheim

In many ways, only Vitesse is interesting enough a football club for Nuon to consider sponsoring. Nuon holds office in Arnhem and, to a much greater extent than any other professional football club in the region, Vitesse stands for flair, innovation, ambition and courage – exactly the kinds of qualities Nuon wants to associate with. In addition, Nuon president Tob Swelheim is charmed by the man widely considered responsible for the reawakening of Vitesse: Karel Aalbers. The appreciation is mutual. Like Aalbers, Swelheim carries out an impressive organisational transformation, turning a local public utility into one of the most valuable organisations in its business. Swelheim is a real fighter, he is energetic, creative, and very intelligent. Swelheim is not an easy person to work with, however. The Nuon president is a typical 'dominant leader' who does not care for others to monitor his activities – including the way he manages the relationship with Vitesse.

In the 1995/1996 season, Ajax shows interest in talented Vitesse player Roy Makaay. Vitesse is all but keen to agree to a transfer. Not only will the transfer sum be limited at this stage of Makaay's career, selling a promising striker to Ajax also undermines Vitesse's attempt to pose a threat to 'the top'. The situation does not just bother Aalbers. Tob Swelheim, who initially took little interest in the actual game itself, has started to like this football thing. He enjoys the Vitesse victories and, perhaps more importantly, defeats get him down. It does not take long for Swelheim to think of himself as a football expert and he is more than willing to share his thoughts with the Vitesse staff. Swelheim openly advises Aalbers to sell Vitesse players or buy players from the team Vitesse is playing against. "Sometimes it was simply too embarrassing to watch", the secretary of the Nuon board of directors recalls, "the board members of the other club could literally hear everything Swelheim and Aalbers discussed. But Tob couldn't care less". Swelheim offers to help Vitesse with the 'Makaay-problem'. The young striker is offered a salary increase and Makaay now earns more money than Ajax would have paid him. Nuon pays for the extra costs by raising its annual sponsoring fee. In addition, Nuon and Vitesse come to an agreement which states that when Makaay is sold at some point in the future, Nuon receives a share of the profit Vitesse makes: ten percent in the first year, twenty percent in the second year, and so on. Swelheim is very pleased with the arrangement and this deal, in which Vitesse cranks up its budget and Nuon takes care of the shortages, is used more often in the future.

Back at Nuon, Swelheim discusses the 'details' of the changing relationship between Nuon and Vitesse with a small group of people only: the other members of the Nuon board of directors, the director of communications and the head of accounting. Aalbers understands that Swelheim, despite his almost absolute power, needs to be able to account for his arrangements with Vitesse: "Swelheim can pull off anything, as long as he is able to present it as a business deal". Aalbers helps Swelheim to do so. When the Makaay-scenario threatens to repeat itself in the case of talented Vitesse player Chris van der Weerden, Vitesse and Nuon agree, again, to the aforementioned financial construction which entitles Nuon to a piece of the transfer profits. Before the agreement takes legal form, however, Chris van der Weerden is sold to PSV. As a token of good will, Aalbers nevertheless decides to 'give' Nuon its ten percent. Swelheim can take this generous offer to the Nuon board of directors and show how profitable this deal really is.

The relationship between Nuon and Vitesse grows more and more intimate and there seems to be no limit to Swelheim's "willingness to advice from a distance". While the Vitesse team does very well in the competition and the Vitesse family grows rapidly, the fruits from this success cannot compensate for all the spending Aalbers does in order to expand even further. In October 1998, Vitesse foresees a shortage of approximately € 11 million at the end of the season. Nuon helps again. It renews the sponsorship contract for another three years and now pays Vitesse € 3,5 million annually – a fee that is comparable to what the top 3 clubs receive from their sponsors. Because Vitesse needs money urgently, Nuon agrees to pay the total sum of money for three years of sponsorship upfront. "We need to win the title", Swelheim makes clear. Business-wise, the deal is considered solid as a rock. At the end of the season, Vitesse will sell star striker and European top scorer Nicos Machlas (estimated transfer sum: € 27 million) and Nuon will get its money back. Should something go wrong, Vitesse would still have to pay interest over the money it borrowed from Nuon. Aalbers, of course, takes great pleasure in Swelheim's growing devotion to Vitesse. The club president often presents new plans to the members of the Vitesse supervisory board. Because a sound financial foundation is usually missing, the supervisory board rarely grants Aalbers permission to carry out his plans. But "at the next meeting Aalbers would calmly inform us that these plans were being executed nevertheless. Aalbers had arranged something with Swelheim", one of the members of the supervisory board recalls. Vitesse's treasurer Henk Brouwer, too, acknowledges that at some point it was simply Aalbers and Swelheim who ran Vitesse. He argues that from the summer of 1999 onwards, "Vitesse was no longer run by its board. Aalbers had found in Swelheim someone to meet his wishes. Aalbers would say: Nuon pays for it" (Henk Brouwer in *De Gelderlander*, 2 December 2000).

The reports on Vitesse's growing dependence on Nuon are important for this study since they provide counterevidence to the Official insistence that Vitesse does not tolerate external influence over its organisation. The image of 'us' versus 'them' just isn't correct – not as far as Swelheim is concerned anyway. One of the moments the Nuon president cherishes most is not the opening night of the Gelredome stadium itself, but the day before it, 24 March 1998. "There were still all kinds of people working. Photographers were walking around. Karel and I were sitting there, having a beer. The feeling of: how marvellous that we managed to accomplish this". Swelheim's choice of words here is important. By explicitly (and repeatingly) referring to a "we", Swelheim refutes the Official claim that Aalbers alone decides how things get organised at Vitesse. The Official understanding of the Vitesse organisation needs probably even more moderation when we consider the effects of the Nuon-Vitesse relationship turning into a Swelheim-Aalbers relationship. Over the years, Aalbers and Swelheim became more than just business partners. "We became buddies, we invited each other to our homes. We were sparring partners, helped one another with problems. [Swelheim] had a delicate health. We supported each other in everything", as Aalbers describes the situation (in *Sportweek*, 19 June 2001). Inevitably, an emerging camaraderie blurs the distinction between expressions of friendship on the one hand and rational business decisions on the other, thereby further blurring the image of "Aalbers runs Vitesse while Swelheim runs Nuon".

The very fact that the question of how things are organised at Vitesse cannot be understood without reference to what Swelheim can do for Vitesse is significant. It is significant because it implies that when Swelheim's position at Nuon changes, the effects of it will echo in the organisation of Vitesse.

### Changes at Nuon, Changes at Vitesse

As argued above, Nuon makes Vitesse a loan under the presumption that the club will be able to acquit the debt once it sells Nicos Machlas. Far from generating the estimated € 27 million, however, the Greek striker is sold for less than € 9 million to Ajax. Vitesse now owes Nuon over € 11 million. Again, Swelheim helps to think up a solution and proposes to convert the loan into a "players foundation". According to the first draft of the plan, Nuon vouches for € 22,5 million in return for which the sponsor receives fifty percent of the transfer profits of all Vitesse players. Because he has gotten used to the idea that the Nuon president can do what he wants, Aalbers believes the agreement is in the bag. But Swelheim warns Aalbers that the situation has changed at Nuon.

Nuon became interested in Vitesse because it felt it needed to prepare itself for the dynamics of an energy market that was soon to be liberalised. As such, sponsoring Vitesse is but part of a more comprehensive programme of 'bracing for the future':

the public utility needs to start to think and act like a proper for-profit company. The main consequence of its 'going commercial' is that Nuon, like any other normal for-profit company, can no longer take its existence for granted. Tob Swelheim concludes that in an open energy market, Nuon is too small to survive on its own. Like any other for-profit organisation that does not want to be put out of business or taken over by larger companies, Nuon looks for companies to merge with, and with good success. For Swelheim, being head of larger company comes with a price. In the old days, the Nuon supervisory board consisted of people who were incapable of crossing Swelheim in any serious way. But with the official ratification of the new Nuon in the summer of 1999, a new supervisory board is installed. Many of the members of this new board are experienced managers who are not easily argued down, for instance when they are unhappy with what has become of the relationship between Nuon and Vitesse. Swelheim realises he can no longer afford to ignore critique concerning his handling of the relationship with Vitesse. The new situation forces the Nuon president to reinterpret what he can do for Vitesse, Swelheim claims to have told Aalbers. "'Karel, we're not that local company anymore'. I was no longer in a position to say 'my share holders want it like this' because they no longer owned the majority of shares. I was willing to help think of solutions, but I could not make the calls anymore. I tried to explain that to Aalbers but he did not believe me". And so, still operating under the assumption that Swelheim, as always, would find ways to finance Vitesse's expansion, Aalbers keeps spending. Disappointed by Aalbers' unwillingness to acknowledge the reality of the new situation (Swelheim: "Aalbers only listens to what you have to say if the message suits his interests"), the Nuon president eventually sees himself forced to part with Aalbers. "That was painful but I had several employees telling me that Aalbers assured them he had arranged something with me, that Nuon would provide the money. I told them that nothing had been agreed to, that we only talked about it".

The relationship between Nuon and Vitesse started out as a relationship between a football club and a (shirt) sponsor. The nature of this relationship changed when Swelheim decided to make Vitesse a loan. Effectively, Nuon had become a bank and Vitesse its client. The initial relationship between Nuon and Vitesse was stretched even further when Swelheim and Aalbers agreed to a deal in which direct investments entitled Nuon to a share of the profits Vitesse made on selling players. In addition to being already a sponsor and a bank, in other words, Nuon had become an investor in a very risky industry. Swelheim's handling of the relationship between Nuon and Vitesse thus had a significant effect on the development of that relationship – an unfortunate effect, Nuon's head of communications Peter Knoers concludes in hindsight. "It is very difficult to draw the line when you are on the move yourself. A situation like this develops step by step. Nuon wanted to be a professional organisation of national and international significance, in the same way that Vitesse reached for the highest in Europe. To enable Vitesse to do so, Nuon invested a large sum of money in Vitesse. In the

1998/1999 season we crossed a limit [when after initial hesitance Nuon decided to pay Vitesse the three years sponsoring fee upfront]. It was an only-once financing. At that point the line between sponsoring and banking blurred, for which we were rightly criticised. [Nuon's] financial involvement became bigger. It was no longer a situation in which we purchased communication activities like shirt sponsoring. It had become more than that. When the plan did not work out, when Machlas did not generate the kind of money we'd hoped for, when other initiatives did not develop according to plan, and when [Vitesse] appeared incapable of paying us back, Nuon was in trouble. We had gotten ourselves into their problems" (Dialoog, 2000). Nuon seeks to undo the changes in the relationship with Vitesse and return to the original arrangement: buy exposure from Vitesse in order to introduce itself to future customers. From September 1999 onwards, and despite Aalbers' attempts to reestablish contact with Swelheim, Peter Knoers deals with all Vitesse issues.

The new situation, of course, has a dramatic impact on Aalbers' capacity to run Vitesse. By and large, Aalbers had only been able to organise things at Vitesse the way he did because of the relationship he had with Swelheim. Nuon's reconsideration of the terms of the relationship, its decision to have Knoers rather than Swelheim handle the new Nuon-Vitesse relationship, and, on top of it all, Swelheim's termination of his friendship with Aalbers, make it impossible for the Vitesse president to organise things the way he wants to. The very fact that decisions at Nuon resonate in the organisation of Vitesse suggests that changes in the organisation of Vitesse are not necessarily reflections of the will of Aalbers. A different example allows this phenomenon to be described in more general terms.

In 1999, Peter Knoers expresses Nuon's concern with the fact that the overall well-being of Vitesse appears fully determined by the functioning of Vitesse president Karel Aalbers. "Suppose [Aalbers] drives his car into a tree. Vitesse has a problem then, but so do we. Aalbers has always been the big engine [behind Vitesse] but it is unbecoming for a company with a turnover of over € 22 million to be this dependent on a single person" (Knoers in *De Gelderlander*, 28 August 1999). This quote is interesting in at least four ways. First, Knoers' telling off Vitesse shows that parties other than Karel Aalbers himself seek to influence how Vitesse is organised. What is even more important, and this will be shown hereafter, is that Aalbers cannot afford to simply ignore these 'external directions'. Second, Nuon apparantly does not care much for Aalbers per se. Officially, the Vitesse organisation is essentially but a means to an end, a tool that Aalbers uses to achieve pre-formulated goals. As far as Nuon is concerned, however, the Vitesse organisation *itself* is what really matters, not Aalbers. Nuon wants the Vitesse organisation to remain functioning, even in the unfortunate case of Karel Aalbers' premature death. In short, Nuon sees the relationship between the Vitesse organisation and Karel Aalbers as the relationship between 'the party Nuon does business with' and 'the person who acts on behalf of that organisation' and not, as the Official Vitesse Story presents it, as the relationship between 'an instrument' and 'the master of the instrument'. Third, in the very same act of confirming that the Vitesse organisation is an actor in its own right, Nuon expresses very specific expectations with regards to the behaviour of the Vitesse organisation. Nuon finds it unsuitable for an organisation as large as Vitesse to be this dependent on the physical well-being of its president. Acknowledging that the Vitesse organisation itself is an actor and telling that organisation how to behave thus go hand in hand. Fourth, the specific expectations Nuon has of the Vitesse organisation appear derived from observations of *other* organisations. Knoers wants the Vitesse organisation to be like organisations that are comparable to Vitesse in terms of, in this case, size. Apparently, 'the other company' is the norm that the Vitesse organisation is expected to conform to.

In what follows I will argue that, far from being an isolated incident, Knoers' attempt to get the Vitesse organisation to be like other organisations is part of a comprehensive programme that 'aims' to render the Vitesse organisation a normal organisation.

## Shaping the Vitesse Organisation

Nuon's attempt 'to sort Vitesse out' and get it to behave like other organisations is not exceptional. What is exceptional is that Nuon makes its expectations explicit and, even more uncommon, that these expectations are communicated in the media. On a day-to-day basis Vitesse faces expectations regarding how it is to go about as a real organisation and in most cases these expectations are not even made explicit: Vitesse is simply expected to behave like a normal organisation.

Even when we limit ourselves to drawing an inventory of the 'material' expectations Vitesse is supposed to fulfil, the list seems endless. Suppose Vitesse is interested to hear what a potential business partner has to offer. Based on his experiences with other companies, this potential Vitesse business partner expects Vitesse to have the facilities that allow him to present his business proposition in a way that is considered normal. This means that Vitesse needs to have a conference room as well as the technical equipment that allows for, say, power-point presentations to be made. If things go well and a business deal is agreed to, the new business partner will want to have someone at Vitesse he can contact for daily business matters (which means Vitesse needs to employ an 'account manager'). The Vitesse business partner will find it reasonable to expect that he can call his account manager (meaning Vitesse needs to get its employee a phone) and given that the business partner cannot be expected to know all the phone numbers of all the people he does business with by heart, he will want to have a business card that has his account manager's phone number on it (and so Vitesse will have to provide for business cards). At some point the business partner will want to be paid for his product, the implications of which are that Vitesse needs a corporate bank account, that it needs to have money in the bank, that it needs an administration system to handle the invoices, and so on. The number of 'material' demands Vitesse needs to meet alone is already large. But on a less material level also, Vitesse faces large numbers of expectations it must fulfil – *must* fulfil because if Vitesse fails to live up to the expectations, it will not be able to establish the business relationships it needs in order to function as a real company. In addition to his material demands, the aforementioned Vitesse business partner will expect (representatives of) Vitesse to behave in a way that is similar to the behaviour he experienced in encounters with other, comparable organisations. The business partner will want to be approached friendly but not too amicably, for instance. And he will expect his Vitesse account manager to respond promptly to the urgent email he sent him. The business partner will expect Vitesse to respect the confidentiality of the signed contract, he will expect Vitesse to pay invoices timely, and he might even expect Vitesse to send him a company Christmas card when the time comes.

Of course, the particular business partner discussed above is not the only person to have expectations regarding the 'behaviour' of the Vitesse organisation. There are all sorts of parties that all have *specific* ideas as to how Vitesse should act. We have seen that a sponsor, for instance, has specific 'sponsor ideas' about what makes Vitesse a club interesting enough to consider doing business with. As for the image Nuon wants to associate with, Vitesse has to be innovative, fun, ambitious and a bit cheeky. If Vitesse fails to live up to those specific expectations, Vitesse simply stops being of use to Nuon. As one of the interviewed Nuon managers phrased it: "we will stay with Vitesse as long as they've got something interesting to offer. If Vitesse becomes a nasty club, for instance because of hooliganism, then that's where it stops". Because Vitesse wants and needs a sponsor like Nuon, the club has no other option but to conform to the image of what Nuon regards as 'an interesting object to sponsor'. Similarly, before it accepts Vitesse as a client, a bank will have Vitesse sign the legal contract the bank has *all* its corporate clients sign. Vitesse cannot but agree to the terms of this contract, simply because Vitesse, as a real company, cannot do without a corporate bank account. And as it accepts these terms, Vitesse becomes like all the other clients banks have. The Vitesse customers have very specific expectations also – expectations these customers consider no more than reasonable given that Vitesse offers itself as the deliverer of a product. A customer wants to be able to make a formal complaint if he is dissatisfied with the Vitesse product, for instance. The customer feels Vitesse should give him this opportunity because making a formal complaint is something that *other* deliverers of products allow him to do also. And because Vitesse wants to be regarded as a reliable deliverer of products, Vitesse sets up a customer relations management infrastructure that facilitates the dealing with disgruntled customers. As a result, in this way also, Vitesse becomes like other organisations.

It is not just external parties that see to it that Vitesse becomes a company that 'is' and 'does' like other, normal companies. In chapter 1 it was argued that in the Official Vitesse Story, the envisioned transition from a football club to a multi-entertainment football company demanded, among other things, a change from working with volunteers to employing professionals. In most cases, people are considered professionals because they have experience, i.e., they have worked in similar positions for other companies. On the whole, these professionals will want Vitesse to be like the other employers they worked for. These professionals will want a salary that is comparable to what other employers would pay them, for instance, and they will want their salary to be paid by the end of every month (and so Vitesse needs to have the resources, the people, the infrastructure, and the software to make that happen). In addition, most of these professionals will want to have someone with whom they can plan their career (and so Vitesse has to set up a Human Resource Management department), some of them will want to have a weekly drink with their colleagues in a relaxed atmosphere (which means Vitesse needs to arrange for drinks and snacks on Fridays), while other Vitesse professionals will argue it is only fair they get to drive a company car (which forces Vitesse to come to an arrangement with a car lease company), and so on and so forth. On a content level as well, in the very carrying out of their jobs, these professionals make Vitesse look like other, normal companies. An account manager who is hired because of the excellent work she has done elsewhere is likely to manage her accounts in a way that is very similar to how she went about in her previous jobs – as she is expected to do. This account manager will approach prospects in roughly the same way she approached potential clients when she still worked for her former boss, she will introduce to Vitesse a policy for dealing with dissatisfied clients she believes has proven to be effective, she will have Vitesse purchase the kind of account management software she has lots of experience with and thus knows to use efficiently, etcetera. In doing so, in modelling 'Vitesse account management' after 'account management as she knows it', the Vitesse employee ensures that in this respect too the Vitesse organisation comes to resemble other organisations.

What to make of these practices that render the Vitesse organisation more and more like other, normal organisations? And, even more importantly, how does the process of 'shaping the Vitesse organisation' relate to an attempt to use concepts from the science of complexity to put some flesh to the idea that organisations live lives of their own? To answer these questions, I turn to the work of Stewart and Cohen (Cohen and Stewart, 1994; Stewart and Cohen, 1997). I will argue that the process of moulding the Vitesse organisation as described above has many similarities with a process these authors describe, and which they believe is fundamental to the coming about of so-called emergent phenomena. I will take the framework Stewart and Cohen have developed to model emergent phenomena and use it to re-conceptualise the Vitesse organisation. After that, I will address the question of what the main consequences are of switching from an organisation-as-tool view to an organisation-as-emergent-phenomenon perspective.

## THE VITESSE ORGANISATION AS AN EMERGENT PHENOMENON

Mathematician Ian Stewart and biologist Jack Cohen are interested in what they refer to as emergent phenomena. The theory Stewart and Cohen have developed for explaining these phenomena is perhaps best introduced by showing what it goes *against*. Stewart and Cohen are dissatisfied with the way one particular group of emergent phenomena, human beings, tend to be conceived of these days. The authors believe "there is a growing, and disturbing, tendency to see the pervasive influence of DNA as *the* major determining factor in the growth and acculturation of a human being: scientists have already announced the discovery of such things as a 'gene for homosexuality' or 'a gene for obesity'. Now there are genes that affect how you behave, or at least how you most easily behave; and studies on identical twins separated at birth show that they have surprisingly similar preferences in many respects. A certain amount of what you are, and what you can be, is 'written in your genes'. But an awful lot more, including almost everything that is culturally and socially important, is not. Most of the special characteristics that make us into distinct individuals result not from biological determinants like genes, nor from the cultural matrix in which we are embedded, but from the complicity between the two" (1997: 265-6; original italics). Stewart and Cohen's notion of complicity is crucial to their theory. The meaning of the concept becomes somewhat clearer in their discussion of what distinguishes the mind from the brain. "How can a conscious, intelligent mind evolve? Instead of giving a reductionist answer based upon the internal fine structure we take an external, contextual view. We see the accumulating knowledge of generations of intelligent beings as a thing or a process with its own characteristic structure and behaviour: extelligence. Extelligence constantly modifies and organises itself through continuing interactions with innumerable individuals. As a result, extelligence has become greater, more permanent, and far more capable than any individual intelligence. However, extelligence makes no sense without intelligences to interact with it: the two are 'complicit'. The developing mind of each child interacts with extelligence by way of language, and the two-way flow between individuals and their surrounding culture changes both. Intelligence is fostered in the child, and extelligence is fostered in the culture. Thus the evolution and structure of the brain cannot be divorced from the evolution and structure of human society and its environment, the universe". The mind, therefore, "is not just a matter of sophisticated brain structure; it is something that arose through the cultural trick of passing on behaviour through teaching and learning. The *contextual* element is crucial: mind cannot arise in isolation" (Stewart and Cohen, 1997: X, 28; original italics).

Concepts like 'extelligence' and 'complicity' allow Stewart and Cohen to propose a very distinct understanding of what it is like to be human. According to these authors, there is more to a human being than its unfolding genetic script. Hence, a theory that focuses exclusively on DNA cannot pass as a theory of human beings. "Nursery tales and puberty rites: these two key ways in which surrounding culture - extelligence - moulds the developing human being are embedded in a mass of other cultural influences. Complicity between the cultured mother and the culture-learning baby is established from the first meeting of their eyes, eliciting the first little smile. Indeed it might go back even earlier, because babies in the womb can hear sounds, and after the gurgling of mother's digestive tract, the thumping of her heart, and the wheezing of her lungs, the next commonest sounds that the baby hears is its mother's voice. The special relationship continues with cuddling, feeding, the sounds that we reserve for making at babies, and special clothing like swaddling and footbinding. There are nappies and medical rituals like vaccination and regular weighing in the special clinic. All of those special influences on the growing child form a matrix of extelligence which moulds the child so that it becomes an effective member of society at any stage of its development. Just as there is a proper succession of clothes worn by the developing child, so there is a succession of cultural matrices to pass through. If four-year-olds are thrown out of the household to scavenge the streets, so be it; and if the ability to read and write is seen as a necessity for economically effective adults, then there will be a special set of humiliations for those who appear not to be getting there in adolescence. Of course none of this works exactly as intended, and it is by no means uniform in its application of its effects – but nevertheless the broad picture applies, all else being equal, across all human cultures. This whole pattern, with universal similarities in all cultures but with enormous parochial differences, is what we shall irreverently call the 'Make-a-Human Kit'"(Stewart and Cohen, 1997: 263). Being exposed to the workings of this Make-a-Human Kit is of vital importance, Stewart and Cohen insist. "Children brought up by animals are not proper people. If that sounds cruel or 'politically incorrect', recall that they cannot learn a language, they cannot reliably respond to a name, and sometimes they have difficulty walking or eating. Such children are genuinely deprived; deprived of the cultural framework of the Make-a-Human Kit. They have the misfortune to belong to a species for whom this kit is as essential as milk, a species that requires a steady supply of cultural input to reconstruct its current level of intelligence in every one of its members. Cut from their Make-a-Human-Kit, they have not been made human" (1997: 267). In other words, according to Stewart and Cohen one is made a human being, rather than born one: a real human being is 'something' that one comes to be, by undergoing the workings of the Make-a-Human Kit. A very similar argument can be made for organisations, I believe.

The analysis of the development of the Vitesse organisation I will offer below rests on the assumption that in the realm of organisations also, it makes sense to presume the existence of a kit with which, in this case, 'real organisations' are made. This Make-an-Organisation Kit is as important to could-be organisations as the Make-a-Human Kit is to the potential human being: in the same way that a child that has been cut from the Make-a-Human Kit fails to become a functional member of *its* society, the Vitesse organisation can only be an effective member of business society if it allows itself to be shaped and formed in the image of "what it is like to be an organisation", to paraphrase Stewart and Cohen (1997: 246).

Earlier I argued that the Vitesse organisation is 'surrounded' by a great many parties, all of them trying to get the Vitesse organisation to resemble other organisations. My claim is that these normalising practices collectively constitute a Make-an-Organisation Kit, a cultural matrix that moulds the Vitesse organisation into a decent organisation. In the following I will further develop the argument that the Vitesse organisation became more of a normal organisation in the course of time. The focus will be on the effects the process of "culturing the Vitesse organisation" has on the relationship between Aalbers and the Vitesse organisation.

## Normalising the Relationship between Aalbers and Vitesse

Nuon was not alone in its demand that Vitesse ought to do something about its 'unhealthy' dependency on its president. Various parties, and for various reasons, criticised Aalbers' firm grip on the Vitesse organisation, deeming it incompatible with normal business practice.

The functioning of an organisation is commonly expected to be insensitive to things that can change from one day to the other. As such, a company's capacity to make business decisions must be immune to, say, the mood swings of the staff. At Vitesse, this was not always the case. In addition to being its president, Aalbers was also a big fan of Vitesse. Not surprisingly then, Aalbers could get genuinely grouchy over a defeat. Therefore, if Vitesse was to play on a Sunday, Aalbers' secretary would not plan any Monday morning meetings – just in case. When Aalbers was in a bad mood, it would also not be unusual for him to disallow people to walk past his room. As a result Vitesse employees would have to take a detour to get to offices further down Aalbers' corridor. As charming as these particular examples may be, they are also indicators of a behaviour that is ordinarily considered unprofessional or abnormal for companies the size of Vitesse. The overall conviction is that the mood of a president should not interfere with normal business processes. Another example of 'inappropriate' behaviour brought up by several interviewees pertains to the ease with which Aalbers would overrule the decisions of others. We have already seen that Aalbers was not too concerned with what the members of the Vitesse supervisory board had to say about the plans he presented to them. It was also not uncommon for Aalbers to brush aside plans contrived by the other members of the Vitesse management team, and go with the plan *he* thought was best instead. A member of the supervisory board remembers one of these events:

"[a manager] decided Vitesse would no longer do business with [company X] so that Vitesse could join hands with [company Y]. Aalbers came along and gave [company X] a second chance. That's how you create agitation in an organisation".

Aalbers did not just overrule others. Over the years, the Vitesse president also managed to develop a reputation as a business partner who would quite easily void deals he had closed himself. Such was the case with the construction of the Gelredome, for example. The envisioned Gelredome stadium demanded the cooperation of a number of constructors. For years these constructors, members of the so-called *bouwcombinatie*, had been developing plans to determine what the Gelredome should look like and how it was to be built. Then, all of a sudden, Aalbers announces he closed a deal with a constructor that had not participated in the *bouwcombinatie*. One of the initial constructors, Gert Bruil, remembers it as follows: "I was informed by chance [about Aalbers' deal with a rival firm] fifteen minutes before the press conference. I was fuming. But hey, that's Karel. He no longer needed us. And then he tends to forget about existing agreements" (Bruil quoted in Van Mierlo, 2001: 80). Broos Swinkels, a representative of beer brewer Bavaria, one of the founders of Gelredome, also experienced Aalbers' opportunistic approach to matters. "With Karel you need to work out every small detail, otherwise he'll make changes to his own advantage. After a year of negotiating, we had finally reached an agreement. Karel was not present when we signed the contract – he was in bed, ill. We sent the contract to Aalbers' home so he could sign it. When the courier returned with the contract, we found out Aalbers had made some changes to it. I find it amusing now because it's typical of Karel but at the time I was furious" (Swinkels quoted in Van Mierlo, 2001: 83).

Stewart and Cohen argue that being moulded by the Make-a-Human Kit ensures that a child remains an effective member of society at *any stage of its development*. By putting it like that, the authors underscore the fact that the shaping of a child in the image of "what it is like to be human" is not a single act and that in each stage of the child's development the question of what it is like to be human is answered differently. A human being is expected to act his or her age and behaviour that is regarded normal in one stage of development does not necessarily *continue* to be considered normal. As a child moves into the next stage of development, behaviour that was once considered appropriate may now be qualified as childish, indecent, irresponsible, inconsiderate or naive. Normality is thus relative, rather than absolute. The same line of argument seems to apply to organisations. It is important to notice that people who criticise Aalbers' behavior often do not condemn it *per se*. A member of the Vitesse supervisory board voices the ambivalence as follows: "when Aalbers wants to go a certain direction, there are very few who can stop him from actually going that direction. Aalbers will talk to a lot of people and then assumes they all agree to what he says. Because of his dominant personality, people are not likely to say 'we should do this differently'. But then again, the fact that he can verbally overwhelm people has brought Vitesse where it is today". In other words, those who question the appropriateness of Aalbers' way of doing business often *also* argue that Aalbers' opportunistic approach to business is exactly what made Vitesse successful in the first place. Still, the 'Aalbers Way' (his tendency to overrule others, his habit of voiding deals that are less appealing in the light of new prospects, his forgetting about partners who failed to remain relevant) slowly stopped being effective and became untenable at some point in time.

As said, the Official Vitesse Story offers the Vitesse organisation as the product of Aalbers' wilful design, construction and control. If we follow the line of argument developed above we come to a rather different understanding of why the Vitesse organisation looks the way it does. When we acknowledge the existence and the workings of the Make-an-Organisation Kit, we accept that there are *many forces* that affect the being of the Vitesse organisation. The 'cultivating organisation' perspective argues that organisations are constantly moulded and shaped in the image of "the normal organisation" – a process that causes these organisations to remain effective members of society at the various stages of their development. Understanding organisations as "products of cultivation" rather than as tools has important consequences, for instance for our explanation of the parting between Aalbers and the Vitesse organisation. Instead of having to accept the Official claim that Nuon robbed Aalbers of his organisation, we can now conceive of Aalbers' involuntary resignation as a form of 'expulsion': in the kind of organisation the Vitesse organisation was slowly developing (moulded) into, there simply was no longer room for someone like Aalbers and it was therefore inevitable that the president would be 'cultured out of' the organisation at some point. This particular line of thought, while potentially very interesting, will not be pursued any further here as it is not the *kind* of argument we are looking for in this study. The reason for this is that there is at least one important assumption underlying the organisation-as-tool view that the theory of 'cultivating organisation' does *not* question, namely the idea that organisation is a passive object. In the analysis offered above, the Vitesse organisation *undergoes* formation, it is *being* shaped, it *gets* moulded. At least for this research, the fact that there is still nothing 'lively' about the organisation is problematic.

The purpose of this study is to develop the idea that organisations live lives of their own. From this it follows that we can neither understand organisation as a bloodless instrument that answers to the will of its owner (the organisation-as-tool view), nor as the effect of a comprehensive 'programme' of normalisation (the cultivating organisation perspective). To answer the question of how to conceive of organisations instead we need to return to Stewart and Cohen's theory of emergent phenomena.

## The Potential Organisation

Thus far, the use of the work of Stewart and Cohen has been limited to a translation of their concept of the Make-a-Human Kit. This kit amounts to nothing by itself, however. In their discussion of the particular emergent phenomenon that is the human being, Stewart and Cohen point out that culture *alone*, of course, is incapable of producing human beings. "Up until now we emphasised the contextual element of human development, but it goes without saying that the development of the embryo/fetus/baby/child/adolescent/adult is also underpinned by the biological machinery of embryology, endocrinology (hormones), physiological growth patterns, development of the brain, and sense organs. You can't make a human from just a Make-a-Human Kit: you need a potential human to apply it to" (Stewart and Cohen, 1997: 265). If we think of organisations as emergent phenomena also, and if we use the framework Stewart and Cohen have developed for approaching these phenomena, the next logical thing to do is to formulate an organisational equivalent of the potential human being. Which, as it turns out, is anything but a simple task.

It is not very hard to picture the potential human being as defined by Stewart and Cohen. The potential human being is that which has the *potential* to become a real human being, but isn't one quite yet. We have seen the authors use the example of children brought up by animals to approximate this potential human being; 'wolfs-children' that do not qualify as proper human beings because they have been cut from the Make-a-Human Kit. Nevertheless, the uncultured corporeality – the potential human being's biological machinery – is 'there', available for us to see and study. If we apply this line of thought to the phenomenon being studied here, it follows that in order to define 'the potential organisation' we need to look at the stuff that organisations are made of. But what *does* an organisation consist of? Is it the people in it? Is it the money that the organisation has in the bank? Is it the buildings and everything in them? And is an intangible asset like goodwill part of the organisation in the same way that a limb is part of a human being? In addition to the problems we encounter in deciding what to accept as the 'building blocks' of organisation, it seems even more difficult to even think of them in a pre-cultured condition. In Stewart and Cohen's framework, the potential human already exists, prior to and independent of its getting cultured[12]. In the case of organisation that line of argument seems much harder to uphold: even if we could formulate a satisfactory definition of the potential organisation, it seems impossible to conceive of that organisation uncultured.

The Official Story tells us that everything the Vitesse organisation consists of is there because Aalbers wants it there. The Gelredome, for instance, is there because Aalbers figured the old Nieuw Monnikenhuize stadium did not contribute to the realisation of the Vitesse Way. In the same vein, professionals are there because Aalbers believed volunteers are incapable of building the Vitesse of Tomorrow.

Officially then, the potential Vitesse organisation consists of only that which Aalbers deliberately put in there. Accepting the cultivating organisation-perspective developed above leads to a different understanding of the 'contents' of the Vitesse organisation. By offering Vitesse as a real company, Aalbers can be said to have (inadvertently) invoked a series of normalising practices over which he has no control. These practices do not merely apply to what already is (forcing Vitesse to change the nature of its workforce, to reconsider the job descriptions of its players, to approach its fans differently, etcetera) but they also determine what Vitesse, as an organisation, should look like *from the very outset*. For example, we expect real organisations to have an office we can visit. Therefore, if Vitesse wants to be thought of as a real company, it simply needs to have an office. In addition, Vitesse needs to have a desk where we can inform the receptionist that we are ready for our eleven o'clock appointment with the facility manager; without a proper reception desk (or a receptionist or facility manager for that matter) Vitesse stands less of a chance being regarded as a real company *and function like one.* As a real company, Vitesse can not afford not to have a coffee machine, or a credit management policy, or an infrastructure for dealing with disgruntled customers, or some sort of security system, and so on. Absent these and many other organisational building blocks, Vitesse will find it very hard to successfully present itself as a proper company. In other words, the Vitesse organisation consists of quite a number of elements that were not deliberately put 'in there' by Karel Aalbers. The Vitesse president was not free to build an organisation from scratch. From the moment Vitesse was re-identified as a multi-entertainment football company, images of "what it is like to be a real company" pervaded the construction process of the New Vitesse, making it virtually impossible for certain organisational elements *not* to be included.

The phenomenon described above affects our ability to formulate an organisational equivalent of the potential human being. Through our imagining of children brought up by animals we can, albeit from a rather dodgy philosophical position, visualise uncultured human beings. Uncultured organisations, on the other hand, are much harder to conceive of as their building blocks are always and already culture-laden. But despite the fact that applying Stewart and Cohen's framework to organisation is not as smooth an operation as one would hope for – the *Make-a-Human Kit* being easier to translate than the *potential human being* – their model of emergent phenomena remains an interesting one. Stewart and Cohen take a contextual view because they are unhappy with 'reductionist' approaches to emergent phenomena. The authors believe that if we continue to see a human being as the sum of its building blocks, we fail to understand human beings *as human beings.* Stewart and Cohen stress that their call for an external view is not an attempt to *replace* studies of the biological machinery with something else: trying to make sense of human beings by analysing the processes of cultivation alone is just as reductionist an approach as is an exclusive focus on a human being's DNA.

The authors' take on matters is perhaps best clarified by their position in the well-known nature-nurture debate. Stewart and Cohen take a rather elusive position in this debate because their aforementioned notion of complicity defies the very polarity that normally characterises the discussion. In archaic discussions, nature and nurture are understood as mutually exclusive sources of order: man is either the product of his inherent, autonomous nature or he is the effect of a moulding and shaping by external (social) forces. In more sophisticated discussions there is room for shared influence, allowing man to be understood as 70 percent genetics and 30 percent environment, for instance. The categorical difference between nature and nurture still remains intact here. But "can the interaction of nature and nurture really be that simple?", Stewart and Cohen ask themselves. As they see it, what accounts for human beings is "not a matter of nature versus nurture, or a mixture of the two, but an integrated, interactive process in which both are intimately related" (Cohen and Stewart, 1994: 306, 378). Because nature and nurture are complicit, the human beings that emerge from them cannot be explained in a reductionist fashion – not by a detailed study of their genetic scripts (nature), not by an investigation of the workings of the cultural matrix in which human beings are embedded (nurture), and not even through a 'mixed reading'. But if not by means of reductionist analysis, how can we study emergent phenomena instead, if at all? According to Stewart and Cohen, the inaptness of traditional research methods does not mean that emergent phenomena are inaccessible to science altogether, "it just means that science must extend its methodology to encompass a theory of emergence". The authors argue that those who acknowledge the reality of emergence are not so-called vitalists who believe that "living material is simply a different kind of stuff from non-living material". But even if, as Stewart and Cohen insist, there is nothing "mystical" about emergence, it is clear that the phenomenon remains very difficult to come to terms with. Emergent phenomena confuse us because "the behavior of the systems seems to transcend that of its parts". But where does the 'excess behaviour' come from? Where to look for the emergent properties? "Where is [the mind]? In the brain? Sure, but *where* in the brain? All over? No, that's no location. But surely if mind exists in a material sense, then it must be *somewhere*? Sounds sensible – until you put your own mind in gear for a moment. Mind is a process, not a thing. Processes take place within things, but they do not have a specific location. Where in a car is its ability to move located? In the wheels? No, because you need an engine too. In the engine, then? No, because you need the wheels. In *both* (along with transmission and so on)? But that's not a location!" (Stewart and Cohen, 1997: 64, 238, 13, 21, 211; original italics).

In the following chapter I will show how Stewart and Cohen deal with the processual nature of emergent phenomena. I will then try to apply their line of thought to organisation and address the question of how understanding organisations as emergent phenomena helps to think of them as living lives of their own.

# 5

# Organisational Aliveness: Seeing Organisations as Emergent Phenomena

## INTRODUCTION

In the previous chapter I argued that Stewart and Cohen's 'potential human being' and 'Make-a-Human Kit' can be translated into organisational equivalents: 'the potential organisation' and 'the Make-an-Organisation Kit'. In this chapter these concepts will be used to develop the idea that organisations live lives of their own.

The particular indicator of organisational aliveness I want to examine here requires that I first discuss how Stewart and Cohen's theory of emergent phenomena relates to other theories of organisation. I will first discuss the work of Stuart Kauffman, who suspects that the "typical properties" of the phenomena he is interested in are reflections of a natural, law-governed order. After a discussion of what the 'Kauffmanian' framework amounts to when we apply it to organisation, I will briefly review the postmodern argument that "typical" organisational properties are best understood as effects of 'discursive production'. I will then link these two schools of thought by means of the work of N. Katherine Hayles, who argues that in spite of the apparent differences between theories of authors like Kauffman on the one hand and certain postmodernists on the other, both traditions share that the importance of a phenomenon's materiality is secondary to that of the underlying abstract mechanism. The contribution of Hayles is particularly interesting for its discussion of the significance of the remainder – the 'stuff' that cannot be logically or discursively addressed. According to Hayles, this residue is important because it has the capacity to destabilise the 'production process' that brought it about. At this point we return to Stewart and Cohen who, like Hayles, argue that living phenomena are more than just expressions or materialisations of a code. Stewart and Cohen use their concept of 'complicity' to show that an emergent phenomenon feeds itself back into the sources from which it sprung, *and changes them*. I will apply this line of argument to the phenomenon we are interested in here, arguing that organisations too change that which forms them. I will then propose to accept this capacity as a sign of organisational life.

## KAUFFMAN AND THE LAWS OF COMPLEXITY

We have seen that one of the key phenomena the science of complexity seeks to address is self-organisation. In chapter 3, self-organisation was theorised in a classical system-environment setting. "The process of self-organisation", Cilliers (1998: 93) writes, is "the result of an evolutive process whereby a system will simply not survive if it cannot adapt to more complex circumstances". This understanding of the nature of self-organisation is not uncontested, however. Stuart Kauffman, for instance, argues that self-organisation is not the outcome of an evolutive process but instead precedes it: "self-organisation may be the precondition of evolvability itself. Only those systems that are able to organize themselves spontaneously may be able to evolve further" (Kauffman, 1995: 185; original italics).

Under the dominant Darwinian world view, Kauffman argues, the great many forms of life have come to be regarded as "incalculable improbable accidents", as "the fruits of ad hocery", or as "historical contingencies" – "Evolution is chance caught on a wing", Kauffman quotes colleague biologist Jacques Monod. Kauffman believes there are serious limitations to what evolution can explain, however, and suspects that life as we know it depends on more fundamental mechanisms: "many features of organisms are not merely historical accidents, but also reflections of *the profound order that evolution has further molded*" (1995: 8; italics added). Kauffman gets his ideas from promising research findings in "the emerging sciences of complexity", which "begin to suggest that the order is not all accidental, that vast veins of spontaneous order lie at hand". If these suggestions are found correct, Kauffman predicts, the consequences will be enormous: complexity science will force us to change the very motto of life from a Darwinian "We the improbable" to a complexity science-informed "We the expected".

Kauffman maintains that when we strive to have fundamental knowledge of "free-living systems", we cannot afford to only pay attention to evolutive processes. He expects to find that "viewed on the most general level, living systems – cells, organisms, economies, societies – may all exhibit lawlike properties, yet be graced with a lacework of historical filigree, those wonderful details that could easily have been otherwise, whose very unlikelihood elicits our awed admiration". In other words, even though the "two sources of order" are "natural partners", life *starts* with a deep and spontaneous order and "it is only then that selection comes into play, further molding and refining" – "the history of life captures the natural order, on which selection is privileged to act". Kauffman believes he knows where this deep order comes from: "laws of complexity spontaneously generate much of the order of the natural world". The author realises his hypothesis is a rather controversial hypothesis. "In considering whether there can be laws of life, many biologists would answer with a firm no. Darwin has properly taught us of descent with modification. Modern biology sees itself as a deeply historical science. Shared features among organisms – the famous genetic code, the spinal column of the vertebrates – are seen not as expressions of underlying law, but as contingent useful accidents passed down through progeny as useful widgets, found and frozen thereafter into that descendant branch of life. It is by no means obvious that biology will yield laws beyond descent with modification. But I believe that such laws can be found" (Kauffman, 1995: 8-71).

Kauffman essentially suggests that the many forms of life we see around us are 'but' earthly variations on a lawlike order. Exactly what these variations will come to look like in the future, he admits, is impossible to predict. "If the origin and the evolution of life is like an incompressible computer algorithm, then, in principle, we can have no compact theory that predicts all the details of the unfolding. We must instead simply stand back and watch the pageant. I suspect that this intuition may prove correct. I suspect that evolution itself is deeply like an incompressible algorithm. If we demand to know its details, we must watch in awed wonder and count and recount the myriad rivulets of branching life and the multitudes of its molecular and morphological details". While Kauffman fears we will never be able to predict the "exact branchings of life", he hopes we can still "uncover the powerful laws that predict and explain their general shape … Even if it is true that evolution is such an incompressible process, it does not follow that we may not find deep and beautiful laws governing that unpredictable flow. For we are not precluded from the possibility that many features of organisms and their evolution are profoundly robust and insensitive to details" (1995: 23). To illustrate what he means by the latter, Kauffman describes the following situation: "when water freezes, one does not know where every water molecule is, but a lot can be said about your typical lump of ice. It has a characteristic temperature, color, and hardness – 'robust' or 'generic' features that do not depend on the details of its construction. And so it might be with complex systems such as organisms and economies. Not knowing the details we nevertheless can build theories that seek to explain the generic properties". And it is generic properties that matter anyway. According to Kauffman, the focus ought to be on "kinds of things", not on details. As such, he believes that he is developing a "fundamental research strategy", one that does not aim to capture all features of living systems, "just those that are fundamentally important" (Kauffman, 1995: 17-9).

Stuart Kauffman is convinced that students of organisation can benefit from complexity science and, in particular, from the *patching procedure* he has developed.

"I suspect that analogues of patches, systems having various kinds of local autonomy, may be a functional mechanism underlying adaptive evolution in ecosystems, economic systems, and cultural systems. If so, the logic may suggest new tools in design problems. Moreover, it may suggest new tools in the management of complex organizations and in the evolution of complex institutions worldwide". Many students of organisation agree with Kauffman (1995: 264-6) that it would be "foolish not to attempt to develop this beginning insight into a rational management technique" and have looked for ways to make use of Kauffman's patching procedure. "Kauffman says break up the organization into patches, yet emphasizes that these patches must interact. This advice is different from the old management standby of the independent, self-sufficient business unit", Lissack writes, for instance (1999: 114). While the patching procedure and its underlying NK-model are undoubtedly worthy of being tested in the realm of organisation, they are not the aspects of Kauffman's work I am particularly interested in. My focus is on the more fundamental claims that the 'Kauffmanian' model makes. What I like best about Kauffman's work is that when we apply it to the phenomena we are interested in here, organisations are said to have generic properties. Under a Kauffmanian world view, the robust properties that define "your typical organisation" are insensitive to details for they are reflections of a spontaneous, law-governed order, an order that "under a vast range of different conditions ... can barely help but express itself" (Kauffman, 1995: 19). The very suggestion that there is a great deal of inevitability to organisations is especially interesting when we confront it with the postmodern critique of the idea that organisations as we know them could not have emerged otherwise.

## The Discursive Production of Organisation

Postmodernists have a very distinct understanding of the relationship between 'the world and the word'. Postmodernism questions the assumption that the world is out there, awaiting our unbiased description of it, and denies that language is an instrument we use to re-present reality as it really is, in and by itself. It maintains instead that language *produces what it denotes*. Chia, for instance, makes reference to the works of French philosopher Jacques Derrida, who writes that "[there] is nothing outside of the text, there is no thingness about the material or social world except when comprehended through the codifying structures of language". Chia concludes from this that "language and words are not wrappings in which things are packed for the commerce of those who write and speak. Social entities, events and things do not first pre-exist and then suffer descriptive distortion through language. Instead language actively configures such entities and events in the very act of representing ... we do not just 'write about' our objects/subjects of analysis. Rather we bring these objects into existence through representational acts of writing" (Chia, 1996: 72).

A postmodern understanding of the relationship between language and organisation leads to a research programme that is quite different from that of 'mainstream' organisation theory. Instead of taking organisations as we know them for granted and try to learn more about them, postmodern organisation theorists focus on the process in which organisation was produced in the first place.

As Cooper and Burrell phrase it, "to understand organizations it is necessary to analyze them from the outside, as it were, and not from what is already organized. It becomes a question of analyzing, let us say, the production of organization rather than the organization of production" (Cooper and Burrell, 1988: 106). Chia puts it as follows: "a postmodern *style of thinking* is one which eschews thinking in terms of accomplishments, of 'nouns', 'end states', insulated, discrete 'social entities' and events ... Postmodern thinking involves a radical questioning of the specialized categories of knowledge which inhabit academic disciplines such as organization studies by attempting to think 'outside' these established disciplines. In so doing it enables us to see that these theories of organization (as institutionalized forms of thought) are always already themselves *effects* of formal organizing processes. For postmodern organization theorists, therefore, 'organization' itself is a *question* and not *yet* a given" (Chia, 1995: 597; original italics). Chia (1996) uses a metaphor to show how the "production of organization" presents us with an end-product that we then needlessly accept as organisation in its essence. He describes this process as a form of 'downstream thinking'. The metaphor begins by arguing there is no such thing as a natural river. It is only when water starts to flow down from the top of the mountain and carves out a path that the contours of a river begin to show. As more and more water flows downwards and further deepens the path, the existing river reaffirms itself, so to speak. However, when we see the water in action, we tend to think that the river was always there and 'naturally so'. The same line of thought applies to organisation. Chia claims that organisations as we know them *could* have emerged otherwise and that their alleged typical properties are but the fossilised effects of a particular discursive production process. That is to say, in the course of time we have come to understand 'organisation as we know it' as 'organisation as organisation is', thereby denying ourselves the opportunity to see that robust properties are not typical of organisation in a 'hard' ontological sense.

A Kauffmanian theory of organisation offers generic properties as reflections of a deep and law-governed order, an order that was bound to come about.

A postmodern take on matters leads to a very different conclusion. Understood as "forms of language" (Gergen, 1992: 207), organisations are not what they are because their being is determined by 'cold', universal laws. Instead, all that we believe is typical of organisations is discursively produced and sustained. Hayles addresses the question of how important a difference this is.

## COMPARING COMPLEXITY WITH POSTMODERNISM

N. Katherine Hayles' interest is in theories of the human being and in particular in contemporary conceptions of 'the body'. Despite the apparent differences between the two research traditions, Hayles sees an important overlap between the works of complexity scientists à la Kauffman who seek to decipher the "universal informational code [that] underlies the structure of matter, energy, spacetime – indeed of everything that exists" and, on the other hand, the writings of those who think in terms of discursive production. According to Hayles, complexity scientists ("the third wave of cybernetics") share with (some) postmodern writers the idea that "the body's materiality is secondary to the logical or semiotic structure it encodes", i.e., the view that "because we are essentially information, we can do away with the body".

Pronouncements of the "postmodern orthodoxy that the body is primarily, if not entirely, a linguistic and discursive construction" are not difficult to find, Hayles shows (1999: 11-2, 192). She points at the work of Baudrillard, for instance, who argues that the "human body, our body, seems superfluous in its proper expanse, in the complexity and multiplicity of its organs, of its tissue and functions, because today everything is concentrated in the brain and the genetic code, which alone sum up the operational definition of being" (Baudrillard, 1998: 18). She refers to the ideas of Kroker and Kroker who she believes "out-Baudrillard" Baudrillard as they rhetorically ask themselves the question: "if, today, there can be such an intense fascination with the fate of the body, might this not be because the body no longer exists?" (Kroker and Kroker, 1987: 20-1). Hayles finds evidence for the erasure of materiality in the work of Haridson also, who imagines "the relation between carbon man and the silicon devices he is creating" to be like "the relation between the caterpillar and the iridescent, winged creature that the caterpillar unconsciously prepares to become" (Haridson, 1989: 335). A similar picture emerges from the research ambitions of Hans Moravec (1988), who dreams of downloading human consciousness into a computer. "Moravec, head of Carnegie-Mellon Mobile Robot Laboratory, has launched a research program that he hopes will make the body superfluous, a chrysalis case to be discarded when our transformation into informational bits is complete" (Hayles, 1993:147-9). At least to some degree, Hayles regards the postmodern version of the "ideology of disembodiment" as a heritage of the works of French philosopher Foucault. "Coincident with cybernetic developments that stripped information of its body were discursive analyses within the humanities, especially the archeology of knowledge pioneered by Michel Foucault, that saw the body as a play of discourse systems" (Hayles, 1999:192). According to Hayles, Foucault's discussions pertain to abstract bodies only, bodies in which "the specificities of their corporealities" no longer play a role. Hayles joins the critics of the Foucaultian body whose universality "is a direct result of concentrating on discourse rather than embodiment" and sets out to put "back into the picture the flesh that continues to be erased in contemporary discussions" (Hayles, 1999: 5, 192-5; for more on the claim that postmodernism "reduces all materiality to linguistic stuff", see Butler, 1993: 27-31).

Hayles' flesh-and-bone counteroffer to the generalised and abstracted body takes form in her discussion of embodiment. "Embodiment differs from the concept of the body in that the body is always normative relative to some set of criteria. To explore how the body is constructed within Renaissance medical discourse, for example, is to investigate the normative assumptions used to constitute a particular kind of social and discursive concept. Normalization can also take place with someone's particular experiences of embodiment, converting the heterogeneous flux of perception into a reified stable object. In a contemporary scientific visualization technology such as positron emission tomography (PET), for example, embodiment is converted into a body through imaging technologies that create a normalized construct averaged over many data points to give an idealized version of the object in question. In contrast to the body, embodiment is contextual, enwebbed within the specifics of place, time, physiology and culture that together comprise enactment. Embodiment never coincides exactly with 'the body,' however that normalized concept is understood. Whereas the body is an idealized form that gestures toward a Platonic reality, embodiment is the specific instantiation generated from the noise of difference. Relative to the body, embodiment is other and elsewhere, at once excessive and deficient in its infinite variations, particularities, and abnormalities". Embodiment "is inherently performative, subject to individual enactments, and therefore always to some extent improvisational. Whereas the body can disappear into information with scarcely a murmur of protest, embodiment cannot, for it is tied to the circumstances of the occasion and the person. As soon as embodiment is acknowledged, [abstractions] disintegrate into the particularities of specific people embedded in specific contexts. Along with these particularities come concomitant strategies for resistances and subversions, excesses and deviations". This latter conclusion in particular makes the distinction between body and embodiment important for this study. According to Hayles, if we think of the spatio-temporal particularities of embodiment that do *not* dissolve into discourse as meaningless side-products, we will be unable to see and account for the "feedback loops between materiality and discourse" (Hayles, 1999: 196-8; 1993: 154-6). This brings us back to the difference between the works of scholars like Kauffman on the one hand and those of postmodernists on the other.

## The Importance of the Remainder

In his discussion of free-living systems, we have seen Kauffman discern between "robust properties" and "historical details". For Kauffman, the difference between the two is a difference of kind, not of degree. Kauffman understands typical properties as reflections of a profound order that constitutes a "stable organization of matter and energy". The details that are produced in the materialisation of this perpetuating pattern he considers largely irrelevant: not only do these details not affect the profound order *itself*, but, and this is of even greater interest to this study, they also leave the *source* of that order intact. Kauffman holds that the laws of complexity he seeks to lay bare have always been around and expects that they will forever govern life the way they have since the beginning of time. There is, in other words, nothing that can change these laws – the laws of complexity are impermeable. As Griffin (2002: 70) puts it: "Kauffman's sense of universals is that of Kant: they are unchanging universal laws. He does not understand these as evolving also". This is exactly where the difference between "law-governed" and "discursively produced" becomes important again.

Hayles maintains that human beings are more than "data made flesh" (Gibson quoted in Hayles, 1999: 5) and believes that a focus on the body at the expense of attention to the particularities of embodiment cannot be justified by an appeal to the inherent blind spot of research on "kinds of things", i.e., by arguing that researchers who are only interested in "your average human being" need not look at the details that a different breed of researchers *is* interested in, namely those researchers whose focus is on "this particular human being" and who therefore *need* to pay attention to the details that make this particular human being special. In Hayles' model, these two different research programmes do not coexist peacefully because details do not necessarily remain details forever. To think of the particularities of embodiment as inconsequential side-products, Hayles contends, is to deny ourselves the opportunity to see that these 'details' carry within themselves the potential of changing the discourse that produces the body in the first place. "It is a truism in contemporary theory that discourse writes the body", Hayles writes. But what is at least as important to acknowledge, she insists, is that the reverse is true just the same. Consequently, we need to address the question of "how the body writes discourse" also and study the process of how "experiences of embodiment bubble up into language" (Hayles, 1993: 163-5). The difference between "law-governed" and "discursively produced" is important because unlike the sealed laws that Kauffman holds responsible for the structuring of life, discourse *can* be penetrated and 'corrupted' by what it brings about. The stuff that exceeds the typical, far more than being filigree that only historians should take interest in, has ways of affecting how life will be ordered in the future.

If we want to theorise the vulnerability of discourse, it makes sense to briefly explore the work of feminist writer Judith Butler. In her discussion of how subjects come to be, Butler writes that "the price of existence is subordination", meaning that being and subjection go hand in hand (Butler, 1997: 20). What is particularly important for our discussion is Butler's insistence that subjects are not formed in a single act. Subject formation, the process of "becoming subordinated by power as well as the process of becoming a subject", is a process that goes on and on and on (1997: 2). Butler's discussion of performativity helps to clarify this point. "In speech act theory, a performative is that discursive practice that enacts or produces that which it names. According to the biblical rendition of the performative, i.e., 'Let there be light!,' it appears that it is by virtue of *the power of a subject or its will* that a phenomenon is named into being". Following Derrida, Butler calls for a different understanding of the performative. Performativity is to be understood, "not as the act by which a subject brings into being what she/he names, but, rather, as that reiterative power of discourse to produce the phenomena that it regulates and constrains" (1993: 13, 2; original italics). For instance, Butler marks the medical interpellation which "shifts an infant from an 'it' to a 'she'" – that is, the very utterance "it's a girl!" – as but the beginning of an ongoing process of subject formation. "But that 'girling' of the girl does not end there; on the contrary, that founding interpellation is reiterated by various authorities and throughout various intervals of time to reenforce or contest this naturalized effect. The naming is at once the setting of a boundary, and also the repeated inculcation of a norm" (Butler, 1993: 7-8). According to Butler, the very fact that the norm needs to repeat itself to achieve its effect leaves that norm vulnerable to being changed *itself*. She writes that "to say that there is a matrix of gender relations that institutes and sustains the subject is not to claim that there is a singular matrix that acts in a singular and deterministic way to produce a subjects as its effect ... Crucially, then, construction is neither a single act nor a causal process initiated by a subject and culminating in a set of fixed effects. Construction not only takes place *in* time, but is itself a temporal process which operates through the reiteration of norms; sex is both produced and destabilized in the course of this reiteration. As a sedimented effect of a reiterative or ritual practice, sex acquires its naturalized effect, and, yet, it is also by virtue of this reiteration that gaps and fissures are opened up as the constitutive instabilities in such constructions, as that which escapes or exceeds the norm, as that which cannot be wholly defined or fixed by the repetitive labor of that norm. This instability is the *de*constituting possibility in the very process of repetition, the power that undoes the very effects by which 'sex' is stabilized, the possibility to put the consolidation of the norms of 'sex' into a potentially productive crises". In short, "these regulatory schemas [of normalisation] are not timeless structures, but historically revisable criteria of intelligibility" (Butler, 1993: 8-14; original italics).

I believe that the ideas of Hayles and Butler make a good introduction to the next discussion, in which we return to the work of Stewart and Cohen. On a very basic level, there are important overlaps between the works of Hayles and Butler on the one hand and those of Stewart and Cohen on the other. Butler, we have seen, speaks of 'girling' – the ongoing and iterative process in which performative acts of all sorts produce real girls. Stewart and Cohen, on their turn, talk about potential human beings, creatures that do not become real human beings unless they are formed and shaped in the normalised image of a proper human being. Furthermore, Stewart and Cohen not only believe that a real human being amounts to more than 'norm made flesh', they also agree with Butler and Hayles that this 'surplus' is not harmless for it has the capacity to destabilise and change that very norm.

## Revisiting Emergent Phenomena

Stewart and Cohen, we have seen in the previous chapter, take issue with authors who draw "a picture of DNA as the Book of Life" and who thus believe that "everything is as it is now because it grew from something in the past that contained, in microscopic form, the entire thing that it now is". Cohen and Stewart stress that "it's not that the program image of DNA is completely false, but the 'program' is only part of the developmental process". To understand human beings in their totality, the authors propose to think of them as *emergent phenomena*, "as philosophers call regularities of behavior that somehow seem to transcend their own ingredients" (Cohen and Stewart, 1994: 288, 426, 290, 232).

While Stewart and Cohen admit they do not yet have a good formal theory of emergence they nevertheless believe they "can pin down some of the general mechanisms that come together to generate emergent phenomena. Among them is our ... concept of 'complicity'". The notion of complicity is grounded in the assumption that because emergent phenomena do not arise in isolation, we can only explain them adequately if we take an external view, "which for want of a better word we shall call 'contextualism'" (1997: 72, 34). Stewart and Cohen realise that scientifically speaking, "context" is a problematic phenomenon. "Reductionist thinking has become very sophisticated over the centuries, and it has acquired a high degree of formalism – for example, the underlying 'laws' are typically stated as mathematical equations. At first sight there can be no such formal structure to contextual thinking: how can we formalise something as nebulous as context? But over the last century science has been moving steadily towards just such a formal structure. The key idea was that the way to understand complicated systems is to embed them in a surrounding 'phase space'" (1997: 48). Developed by mathematician Henri Poincaré, the concept of phase space has led to today's geometric approach to dynamical systems. "The geometry of dynamical systems takes place in a mental space, known as phase space. It's very different from ordinary physical space. Phase space contains not just what happens but what might happen under different circumstances. It is the space of the possible". Put differently, a "phase space includes not just the *actual* values of the state variables, but all the *potential* values: it is a formalisation of the notion of context" (Cohen and Stewart, 1994: 200; Stewart and Cohen, 1997: 49; original italics). A phase space allows us to think, for instance, not only of creatures that already exist, but also of the ones that *could* exist – 'creature phase space' or 'creature space' contains *all* possible creatures. "Creature space possesses its own geography, and large parts of the landscape are uninhabited. Viable creatures concentrate around particular areas; one is labeled 'hummingbirds,' another 'horses.' In between come portions of creature space that correspond to hummingbirds with tiny hooves, or horses that hover in midair and suck nectar" (Cohen and Stewart, 1994: 372). Of course, creature space is not the only phase space there is. There is also DNA space, for example. "DNA sequences live in DNA space, and in the absence of any other influences would wander around dynamically through the geography of DNA space, seeking attractors ["the things that the dynamics converge toward if your wait long enough"] and settling on them. Similarly, organisms live in creature space, and in the absence of any other influences would wander around dynamically through the geography of creature space, seeking attractors and settling on them. However, there are other influences, which couple those two spaces". When different phase spaces are combined, interesting things happen. New phenomena emerge. "For example, let's think about the transmission of malaria by a mosquito. Malaria is caused by a parasite that lives in human blood. Mosquitoes suck blood and inadvertently ingest the parasite as well. Then, when they attack another human being, they can pass the parasite on. What is special about this kind of system is that the interaction between several subsystems *enlarges the space of the possible*. There is nothing remotely like malaria in blood space, or in bloodsucker space. But when those two spaces interact, they open up entirely new possibilities. The flight of mosquitos wasn't invented to transmit malaria; when flight evolved the malaria parasite didn't exist, because people didn't. Blood wasn't invented as food for mosquitoes; that was an earlier explosion of the space of the possible, with bloodsucking insects evolving because there was blood around to suck. Put all the bits together – bloodsuckers, flight, multiple hosts – and you *still* haven't caught any glimpse of parasites in the combined space of the possible. Wait, though, and they emerge from the new interactive dynamic" (Cohen and Stewart, 1994: 414-9, 206; original italics). Malaria, in other words, wasn't already there, awaiting the right moment to actualise itself. Instead it emerged as a brand new phenomenon, as an effect of the complicity of multiple phase spaces. Similarly, recall that according to Stewart and Cohen, "most of the special characteristics that make us into distinct individuals result not from biological determinants like genes, nor from the cultural matrix in which we are embedded, but from the complicity between the two. Complicity generally implies new, unexpected phenomena, which is why – to pick examples at random – in the UK so many bus drivers have close forebears from the Indian subcontinent, and a huge number of fish-and-chip shops are run by Cypriots" (1997: 266). Like malaria, these specific emergent social phenomena simply did not exist prior to the coupling of spaces. "It is easy to fall into the trap of assuming that nothing can come into being without precedents. If so, everything that is around now must trace back almost indefinitely. However, emergent phenomena do not possess rudiments: that is what makes them emergent", Stewart and Cohen write (1997: 221).

Perhaps the best way to determine the value of Stewart and Cohen's theory of emergent phenomena is to compare it to the work of Kauffman. The concept of complicity was derived from a recombination of the words *complexity* and *simplicity*. In that process of playing with words, Stewart and Cohen invented another concept also: simplexity. "We shall give the name 'simplexity' to the process whereby a system of rules can engender simple features. Simplexity is the emergence of large-scale simplicities as direct consequences of rules". What is characteristic of simplexities is that properties are direct and inescapable consequences of rules. "An important point about simplexities is that their presence is guaranteed, once you have the rules. Any system with the same rules will necessarily exhibit exactly the same simplexities ... Simplexity, then – either in nature or in theoretical models – is the emergence of simple features as a direct (though possibly highly intricate) consequence of 'deep down' rules" (Cohen and Stewart, 1994: 411-4). This is very reminiscent of what Kauffman proposes. Stuart Kauffman argues that our primary interest should be in "robust features" and the universal laws that brought them about. That is exactly what Cohen and Stewart 'hold against' think tanks like the Center for Complex Systems or the Santa Fe Institute of which Kauffman is a member. In a section subtly entitled *reductionism plus?*, Cohen and Stewart write that "the main point we would make about their brainchild, complexity theory, is that it is a theory of simplexity; complicity isn't even in the picture" (1994: 441-2). According to Kauffman, the features that matter are the ones that are direct consequences of rules. Hence, when you know the rules, you know what to expect. This promise of an outlook on 'knowledge of the future' is missing in Stewart and Cohen's theory of complicity. Since rules are not presumed fixed here, knowledge of these rules has limited future value only. The very notion of complicity undermines the hope that underneath the proliferation of life forms lies a code that, once cracked, enables us to predict the core properties of phenomena that are yet to emerge. Stewart and Cohen's model of complicity has no such constant built into it – "one of the universal features of complicity is the emergence of new patterns, new rules, new structures, new processes that were not present, even in rudimentary form, in the separate components" (1997: 245).

## A Natural Organisational Order

How is the preceding discussion relevant to the development of the idea that organisations live lives of their own? We have seen that a Kauffmanian understanding of organisation renders its "core body" a reflection of spontaneous, law-governed order. The idea that organisations will sooner or later be ordered by forces that go beyond the specifics of the individual situation echoes in various discussions of the development of the Vitesse organisation.

The CEO of a Dutch top 3 football club I interviewed, admitted being impressed by what Vitesse had achieved at the time of the interview, which took place prior to the discharge of Aalbers. "Vitesse is an ambitious, opportunistic club. They are taking it to the max and so far they got away with it. Karel Aalbers is prepared to take big risks and he has done a great job". At the same time, the interviewee questioned the tenability of Vitesse's business model. "Vitesse does things it cannot afford. Vitesse has too many employees. [Our club] couldn't afford the number of people working at Vitesse's communication department. I know how much things cost in this business and I know how much sponsors are prepared to pay. Aalbers takes many risks. Take Nuon, for example. If Nuon appoints someone who revises the sponsorship, the whole thing could collapse ... Vitesse is not run like a professional organisation. The way Aalbers goes about won't last forever. Football clubs are becoming more and more like normal companies. They have a supervisory board, a CEO who knows about business rather than football, and so on. The Karel Aalbers type will become a dinosaur ... Football is no more complicated a product than any other: every industry has its peculiarities and risks but normal business processes apply here just the same". In short, this interviewee argues that Vitesse is unable to withdraw itself from the overall trend of football clubs turning into normal organisations. As a result, the Vitesse organisation becomes susceptible to the principles and processes that apply to all normal organisations. Therefore, if one aims to predict what the Vitesse organisation will look like in the future, one has to look beyond the spatio-temporal specifics of the Vitesse organisation and think of the latter, first and foremost, *as an organisation.*

A similar picture emerges from Jos Vaessen's perception of the discharge of Karel Aalbers. Vaessen, Aalbers' successor as president of Vitesse, does not believe that the course of events was unique in any way. Rather than going into the specifics of the situation – such as the fact that we are dealing with a football club from Arnhem, the fact that the person who got fired was Karel Aalbers, or the fact that Nuon was involved in this process – Vaessen discusses matters in very general terms. According to Vaessen also, Vitesse is first of all *an organisation*, which means that general knowledge of "your typical organisation" can be used to make sense of it. "From what I've heard, everything [at Vitesse] went through one channel: Karel Aalbers. That is both the strength and the weakness of an organisation: the high ranking on the league table and the realisation of the Gelredome show the strength of it. The weakness of it has become apparent in today's financial situation. Creative people, people who are determined to make something happen are rarely the kind of people who can place things under control. That is the dualism because without Aalbers, Vitesse would probably still be in the first division. The problem with visionaries is that they are so focussed on their ideas that they lose sight of reality and fact and fiction merge. Somewhere in that process things derailed. My task is to burst the bubble and get Vitesse back to reality" (Vaessen in *Voetbal International*, 26 July 2000). Vaessen thus believes that one can make sense of organisational developments at Vitesse without paying too much attention to all the details that make Vitesse look unique: when you realise that Karel Aalbers is a creative visionary, and when you realise that the Vitesse organisation was becoming more of a mature organisation, then your knowledge of 'organisations in general' allows you to predict that the position of Aalbers would become problematic at some point.

According to the sort of argument these two interviewees put forth, the developments that took place at Vitesse were really not all that spectacular: if you wait for the effects of the intense media coverage to wear off and focus on the essence of the situation, you will find that Vitesse is just another organisation that got 'straightened out'. That is, if one scratches the surface one will find that underneath all that makes Vitesse look special lies a core phenomenon that is insensitive to details – a robust body, the workings of which we can predict because of our general knowledge of organisations. The details of the situation may matter to those who take a special interest in Vitesse, but they count for little to researchers who are interested in the deep nature of organisations. Put differently, according to this line of reason, the stuff that remains behind when we abstract the Vitesse organisation into your typical organisation is effectively harmless: the details make a tame remainder that has no other value than that of food for historians – people who want to find out what *exactly* happened at Vitesse.

In the case of simplexity, a fundamental understanding of the particular complex systems that are organisations 'merely' requires knowledge of the deep laws of complexity. Complicity does not work like that. The emergent phenomena that complicity generates cannot be understood as materialisations of abstract scripts. Stewart and Cohen (1994: 426) go against authors who suggest that knowledge of the human being follows directly from information about its genetic code because DNA supposedly "contains a tiny coded version of a complete man or woman". Stewart and Cohen also deny that humans beings are cultures-made-flesh, which would imply that an understanding of human beings can be derived from knowledge of human culture. Below I will try to apply Stewart and Cohen's non-reductionist theory of emergent phenomena to organisation. The discussion will focus on the question of how to avoid treating organisations as expressions of the Make-an-Organisation Kit.

## The Emerging Organisation

A critique of the idea that organisations are but expressions of the Make-an-Organisation Kit could start with developing Stewart and Cohen's acknowledgement that the cultural matrix is "by no means uniform in its application of its effects". References to *the* Make-an-Organisation Kit may invoke the incorrect image of a coherent, internally consistent, and centrally coordinated regulatory scheme. The counterargument can be borrowed from Foucault, who, in his discussion of the "political technology of the body", writes that "of course, this technology is diffuse, rarely formulated in continuous, systematic discourse; it is often made up of bits and pieces; it implements a disparate set of tools or methods. In spite of the coherence of its results, it is generally no more than a multiform instrumentation. Moreover, it cannot be localized in a particular type of institution or state apparatus ... What the apparatuses and institutions operate is, in a sense, a micro-physics of power" (Foucault, 1995: 26). In addition we have Butler pointing out that normalisation does not happen in a single act: the norm needs to repeat itself to achieve its effect. A very similar argument was made in our discussion on the formation of organisations. The normalisation of the Vitesse organisation involves large numbers of different parties, each of them literally minding their own business as they shape the Vitesse organisation. There is no central coordination of activities, not even a common goal. The banks Vitesse does business with, for instance, are particularly if not exclusively interested in the behaviour of Vitesse as the client in the bank-client relationship. In the end, the bank merely cares about the question of whether or not Vitesse can redeem the loan. In order to minimise the risk of losing money, the bank thinks up all sorts of terms and procedures that Vitesse cannot but accept if it wants to function like a proper company. Effectively then, the bank regulates only that 'part' of the Vitesse organisation that it takes interest in. The very same line of argument applies to the various other parties Vitesse does business with: customers, the supervisory board, the local government, suppliers, insurance companies, sponsors, the press, employees, and so on – all these parties seek to shape particular aspects of the Vitesse organisation in a way that suits *their* interests. Instead of a grand design, there is this particular account manager of this particular bank discussing the options with this particular individual in the financial department at Vitesse, this member of the supervisory board complaining about Aalbers' behaviour to this member of the Vitesse management team, this sponsor asking this safety coordinator what Vitesse plans to do about the outbursts of hooliganism, this employee trying to arrange a meeting with her supervisor to discuss her career options, and so on. There is, in other words, no master plan that is used to render the Vitesse organisation a real organisation: the cultivation of the Vitesse organisation takes place in local interactions, through micro-practices of normalisation. The fact that it is these *local interactions* that matter becomes apparent when we look into Stewart and Cohen's claim that emergent phenomena are not just interesting in themselves.

## How Emergent Phenomena Change the Setting

When the Make-a-Human Kit 'installs' itself, it does more than just convert potential human beings into proper human beings. One could argue that when a culture applies itself to human beings, generation after generation, it catapults itself into the future. Stewart and Cohen point out that the process in which cultures reinvent themselves forward, so to speak, is not free of 'errors'. "Cultures are not replicative systems, but reproductive ones. They do not copy themselves inflexibly from each generation to the next: they modify themselves" (Stewart and Cohen, 1997: 287). The distinction between reproduction and replication is both real and important, the authors insist. "Scientists are so impressed by the manner in which DNA replicates that they tend to see it as the archetypal self-replicating system. However, Richard Lewotin has pointed out that whatever DNA is, it is not *self*-replicating. Putting some DNA in a test tube and waiting for it to replicate is comparable to laying a letter down on a desk and waiting for it to copy itself. The letter needs a photocopier before it can replicate, and the DNA needs a fully functioning cell. There are millions of copies of the same document lying around, and biologists are reading it intently in the hope of understanding how it copies itself. Meanwhile the photocopier in the corner sits neglected and forlorn" (Cohen and Stewart, 1994: 294). Stewart and Cohen thus deny that the fully functioning cell the DNA uses to copy itself can be thought away after the replication has taken place. The photocopier remains in the picture because, as it turns out, it does not always make perfect copies of the DNA; replication often 'degenerates' into reproduction. "Although the loop formed by DNA and its support team is in principle replicative, in practice it is 'only' reproductive. The procedure is so complex that it seldom takes places without errors. Moreover, in sexually reproducing organisms, the reproductive procedure introduces 'mix-and-match' modifications. This should not be thought of as a defect. Reproductive systems are much more interesting than mere replicative ones, precisely because they change. Replication is just the same thing repeated forever. Reproduction has room for flexibility" (Stewart and Cohen, 1997: 18).

As said, Cohen and Stewart believe that the Make-a-Human Kit is a reproductive system as well. A culture that applies itself to human beings gets changed *itself* in the process also because human beings 'fail' to make perfect copies of the original culture. "Our cultures are not fixed: they are recursive. Each generation re-creates its culture in the likeness of that passed on to it by the previous one. However, this re-creation is not exact – the cause of much parental *angst*. We re-create our cultures *flexibly*" (Stewart and Cohen, 1997: 272; original italics). The fact that human beings are more than just the disinterested couriers of a culture is relevant for this study. One could argue that the fact that human beings *embody, live and change* their cultures us an indicator of the aliveness of these human beings. The more children stop to blindly accept being fed this, being dressed like that, or being treated like this, i.e., the more they stop being passively moulded and formed, the more we think of them as living lives of their own. In the process of resisting formation, they *change* the Make-a-Human Kit: by not eating this, they change food culture; by not wearing that, they change fashion; by refusing to be treated this way, they change social life, etcetera. The capacity of human beings to 'change that which forms them' contributes significantly to their being regarded as emergent phenomena. In Stewart and Cohen's model, human beings are phenomena that emerge from the complicity between biological determinants and the cultural matrix. As an emergent phenomenon, a human being is not only not *reducible* to the sources from which it sprung, it also changes them – the UK bus drivers with close forebears from the Indian subcontinent or Cypriot fish-and-chip shops owners *change* the culture in the United Kingdom (and may, in the long run, even contribute to genetic changes; see Cohen and Stewart, 1994: 314). I believe that a similar argument can be made for organisations.

## ORGANISATIONS: LIVES OF THEIR OWN

In chapter 3 I tried to show that organisations can be attributed the ability to learn. If that attribution 'sticks', I claimed, it may contribute to our thinking of organisations as living entities. The same line of thought applies to the capacity to "change that which forms you". If we apply the argument developed above to organisations it not only follows that real organisations are more than expressions of the Make-an-Organisation Kit but also that organisations feed themselves back into that kit, thereby re-creating it flexibly. Like the notion of organisational learning (systemic learning that does not depend on the learning capacities of the people inside an organisation), the very idea that organisations, as emergent phenomena, can change the culture that renders them proper organisations is still largely under-theorised. Similar to what I did with the concept of organisational learning in chapter 3, I will discuss some of the main conceptual implications of formalising the idea that emerging organisations change the Make-an-Organisation Kit that allowed them to emerge.

In an earlier discussion I argued against a mechanistic understanding of the process of culturing organisations. I claimed that there is no such thing as a coherent culture that forces itself upon organisations, instantly leaving the potential organisation a proper organisation. The deceptively clear image of *this thing changing that thing* also needs to be rejected when we visualise organisations feeding themselves back into the Make-an-Organisation Kit. Above it was argued that the cultivation of the Vitesse organisation takes place in local interactions: this account manager of this bank discussing the terms of the relationship with this specific manager at Vitesse, this employee in this department discussing her career options with this supervisor, this sponsor complaining to this member of Vitesse's supervisory board, and so on. These interactions are exactly inter-actions because the moulding and shaping of the Vitesse organisation amounts to more than just 'moves inwards'. Any of the local attempts to turn Vitesse into a decent employer, client, brand recognition generator or deliverer of services is but the starting point of an ongoing process of requests and responses, offers and counteroffers, actions and reactions. A process that never comes to a stop, as Stewart and Cohen point out. "Things interact when one of them affects the other. Once. Things are complicit when their interactions change them, so that soon they have become different things altogether – and *still* they continue to interact, and change, and interact again, and change again ..." (1997: 63; original italics). Thus, trying to say something intelligible about how the emerging Vitesse organisation changes the Make-an-Organisation Kit is not only difficult because it is not a matter of 'this changing that' but also because the changes never solidify. But even if they did, even if changes would settle down as fixed effects in the Make-an-Organisation Kit, then the nature of local interactions in emergent phenomena would still deny us the opportunity to associate them with specific causes. For one thing, interactions do not take place in isolation: the relationship between Aalbers and Nuon president Tob Swelheim affects the relationship between Aalbers and his managers, which, in turn, affects the relationship between managers and the rest of the Vitesse staff, which affects the quality of the work of these employees, which affects the image of Vitesse, which affects the chances of talented players signing a contract with Vitesse, which affects the results of the squad, and so an so forth. Cross-interactions influence (reinforce, moderate, accelerate, slow down) the relationship between an input and an output. The fact that we have no way of knowing in advance what *sort* of effect other interactions will have on a certain relation, let alone to what degree, makes it impossible to highlight an effect (a specific change in the Make-an-Organisation Kit) and find a cause for it (a certain action at Vitesse). This is all the more the case because the Vitesse organisation, of course, is not the only phenomenon to have an effect on the Make-an-Organisation Kit: virtually anything can influence the cultural matrix, which means that in all but extreme cases, changes in the Make-an-Organisation Kit cannot be unequivocally ascribed to the emerging Vitesse organisation.

The last point I want to make is probably the most fundamental one. In chapter 4 I argued that it is not possible to conceive of raw, unshaped organisations. Because images of 'what it is like to be an organisation' play a vitally important role in the emergence of real organisations, organisations as we know them are always and already culture-laden. Moreover, organisations are not shaped by external forces only. A fundamental and categorical difference between the Vitesse organisation and the Make-an-Organisation Kit is impossible to maintain because the Vitesse organisation is as much cultured *from within* (by its employees, by the software it uses, by its corporate furniture) as it is moulded by forces 'out there'. In other words, the Make-an-Organisation Kit cannot be safely assumed external to the Vitesse organisation, culturing the latter from a distance. The distinction between organisations on the one hand and the Make-an-Organisation Kit on the other is thus an artificial, heuristic distinction: in reality the two cannot be separated from one another. This point relates to Cohen and Stewart's admission that individual phase spaces like "DNA space" or "creature space" do not actually exist. "Don't be confused by this image. Several billion years of evolution have bound our present DNA space and creature space altogether, and a combined dynamic has settled out. As a result, we never see individual dynamics of 'naked' DNA space or 'naked' creature space" (1994: 421-2 original italics). When DNA space and creature space are already bound together, the question of how and to what extent they influence each other becomes impossible to answer. The same applies to organisations and the Make-an-Organisation Kit. Like organisations, the Make-an-Organisation Kit can not be thought of naked: without organisational material to 'feed on', there could have never been a cultural matrix that transmits what it is like to be an organisation. If the "organisation space" and "culture space" already imply each other, we have no way of determining how and to what extent an emerging organisation changes the Make-an-Organisation Kit (and vice versa, of course).

We will never know precisely what effect the emergence of the Vitesse organisation has had on the Make-an-Organisation Kit. Maybe the stormy success of Vitesse has affected our appreciation of people like Karel Aalbers. If this is the case, then the emergence of the Vitesse organisation can be said to have prompted changes in the specific part of the Make-an-Organisation Kit that is 'the general opinion about strong leaders'. Maybe there is a teacher in a management school who, after having read reports on the development of the relationship between Vitesse and Nuon, felt she needed to redesign her course on 'strategic corporate alliances', thereby changing that part of the Make-an-Organisation Kit that is 'management education'. Maybe the Nuon-Vitesse relationship will motivate some legislator to try and pass a law that regulates the sponsoring activities of public utilities, thus changing the legal aspects of the Make-an-Organisation Kit. Who knows. The Make-an-Organisation Kit is an emergent phenomenon and as such, by definition, we will never be able to pin it down and find out exactly how and why 'it' developed they way it did. Still, as is the case with other life forms, the fact that we are unable to blame a specific organisation for a specific change in the Make-an-Organisation Kit needs not stop us from thinking of organisations as living lives of their own.

## In summary

In chapter 3, the attempt to use complexity science to (further) develop the idea of organisational aliveness took place in a 'classical' system-environment setting. In this chapter, a different and arguably more experimental route was taken. First I discussed the work of complexity scientist Stuart Kauffman, arguing that from a Kauffmanian point of view, the typical properties of organisations need to be regarded as reflections of a natural, law-governed order. Via N. Katherine Hayles and Judith Butler I then turned to the writings of Stewart and Cohen. These authors contend that emergent phenomena are not direct and inescapable consequences of some form of code. Truly emergent phenomena result from complicity. Understood as emergent phenomena, organisations are not only irreducible to either one of the sources from which they sprung, they also *change* the latter. I argued that an organisation's capacity to change the Make-an-Organisation Kit can be interpreted as a sign of organisational life but at the same time I concluded that attempts to develop this capacity in greater detail is likely to strand in conceptual problems of various kinds.

6

# Conclusions

In this book I have tried to put some body to the idea that organisations live lives of their own. My trying to conceive of organisations as living entities needs to be distinguished from other, seemingly similar attempts to render organisations alive. It is different from the work of Arie de Geus, for example, whose understanding of "the living company" follows from research on "corporate longevity", i.e. on the question of what makes "long-lived companies" so successful (De Geus, 1997). My attempt to think of organisations as living their own lives is also not a spiritualist call for the "return to ancient wisdom, supposedly now made scientific by complexity sciences", as Griffin (2002: 85) characterises Wheatley's (1993) effort to describe organisations as "living systems". In chapter 1 I argued that my ambition to develop the notion of "organisational aliveness" needs to be understood as a counteroffer to the idea that organisations are lifeless objects. For this reason I first constructed the organisation-as-tool view, which says that organisations are instruments that amount to nothing by themselves, derivatives that exist by the grace of man and his goals. I argued that in order to theorise organisational aliveness I would seek help from the "New Science" of complexity and the material (ideas, concepts) it offers to question the three main assumptions underlying the organisation-as-tool view: there can be no organisation without an organiser; an organisations is always there for an external reason; the structure of an organisation reflects the conscious decisions of the organiser.

In chapter 2 I showed that applying complexity theory to organisation does not necessarily lead to the particular research project I want to carry out; I am but one of many students of organisation who believe that 'this complexity thing' has something to contribute to the field of organisation and management. Students of organisation have turned to complexity for various reasons: while some authors wanted to see if complexity theory helps CEOs build more competitively advanced firms, others have studied the works of complexity scientists to find out if complexity forces us to rethink our approach to the knowledge creation process in organisations, or if it leads to a different appreciation of resistance to organisational change, if it sheds a new light on the capacity of companies to innovate, and so on. What is interesting to notice is that in the application of complexity concepts to organisation, the "revolutionary" potential of the New Science often gets tamed.

## Taming Complexity

Take self-organisation. Self-organisation is a rather disturbing phenomenon, as Stewart and Cohen point out: "our intuition is upset by self-organisation, probably because we seldom experience such behaviour directly: in our everyday world the only way to produce organisation is to work pretty damned hard to make it come about" (1997: 14-15). It seems safe to argue that in the world of management and organisation, the very idea that 'stuff could organise itself' does more than just upset the intuition – it threatens the very foundations of the field. As such, one would think that 'management thinkers' like Thomas Hout (1999) have good reasons to respond to the growing interest in complexity by re-legitimising management and defend it against the suggestion that self-organisation would make managers obsolete. However, a quick scan of actual attempts to apply complexity to organisation reveals that management has little to worry about for no author on the subject of "complexity science applied to management and organisation" dares to suggest that the era of management has come to an end. At the most, complexity science is interpreted as a call for us to start organising *differently*.

Lewin and Regine, for example, ask leaders to think through the ramifications of complexity research. They argue that this process begins "with nothing short of a personal conversation, that is, a difficult and often painful process of learning to let go of the illusion of control ... It entails a reflection on yourself; placing aside ego-driven needs and instead finding gratification and satisfaction in cultivating others; it's embracing the leader as a servant" (2000: 264). Contrary to what Hout fears may result from the growing enthusiasm over complexity theory, Lewin and Regine do not claim that to accept the reality of a phenomenon like self-organisation is to do away with management altogether. The authors understand 'the capacity to organise itself' in a way that can hardly be said to undermine the need for management *per se*. Regine and Lewin interpret self-organisation as the ability of employees to take meaningful action, even in the absence of clear instructions. "At Monsanto, CEO Bob Shapiro had to make his organization unsuccessful in the way it functioned in order for internal patterns to break down. He overloaded the business with impossible demands, so that people had to discover for themselves a new way of working together; that is, by self-organizing around the most immediate problems" (Regine and Lewin, 2000). When put like this, self-organisation does not pose a threat to management as such. Quite the contrary: the ability of organisational elements to organise themselves becomes an *asset*, something that management can act upon. And this is exactly what successful leaders do. "All the leaders [Regine and Lewin interviewed] saw the workplace as an experiment in progress. In order to stimulate self-organization and a new way of working, they needed to develop trust, which led them counter-intuitively to create chaos in varying degrees, which broke down the existing structures. Working with nonlinear processes led them to see relationships as a new bottom line. Their simple rules from which complexity emerged were values creating a strong ethical foundation that provided continuity in times of uncertainty and flux. These values cultivated conditions for a culture of care and connection to emerge that made the organizations more adaptable" (Regine and Lewin, 2000).

The way students of organisation have treated complexity science thus far is not fundamentally different from how they have welcomed other 'alien theories'. In chapter 2 it was argued that shortly after its introduction in the field of organisation and management, culture came to be regarded as a possession, as something that management can place under control and make use of (Jeffcutt, 1993: 26). Complexity seems to have 'fallen victim' to the same procedure. Like "corporate culture", complexity has already come to be understood as something that is manageable – or can be made so. Complexity is typically seen as something that organisers can include in their "sphere of control" (Stacey, 2001: 3). Regine and Lewin are not alone to suggest that the phenomena complexity theory describes are there for leaders to "stimulate", "create" or "work with". Most authors on the subject assume that complexity is susceptible to managerial action: we can "use complexity", make it "work for us" (Axelrod and Cohen, 2001), we can "manage complexity" (Lissack and Gunz, 1999), we can "unleash the power of complexity" (Lewin and Regine, 1999), we can take the "lessons from complexity science" and use them to "create quantum organizations" (Youngblood, 1997), to "shape the adaptive organization" (Fulmer, 2000), to "change conversations in organizations" (Shaw, 2002), to "facilitate organizational change" (Olsen and Eoyang, 2001), to "help your business achieve peak performance" (Kelly and Allison, 1999), and so on.

Concepts like self-organisation, chaos or emergence are rarely used to question the image of 'organisers in control of organisations'. If anything, a firm knowledge of complexity is said to enable a manager to fasten his grip on the organisation – even though it may take the form of the paradoxical advice to "let go". As such, I believe that the reception of complexity theory bears testimony to a more general phenomenon: while we are willing to accept that new theories may force us to reconsider exactly *how* we are to organise, we are not very likely to challenge the assumption that we *can* organise. This primacy of human agency in our thinking of organisations has important consequences for the popularity of theories that question the assumption that organisations are there for us to manage, as e.g. population ecology theorists found out. As Grandori (1987) sees it, population ecology theories of organisation are "logical extensions of systems and contingency theories", discussed in chapter 3. According to Shafritz and Ott, "population ecology theorists are concerned with competition, selection, and survival of the fittest in populations (groupings) of organizations ... Population ecology theory of organizations assumes that natural selection processes operate among organizations. Organizations do no adapt to their changing environments by making decisions; instead the environment selects among organizational forms" (Shafritz and Ott, 1992: 267). It is exactly this presumption of a "determining force of environmental necessity as an explanation for structural change", i.e., the emphasis on the importance of forces over which man has no control that the critics of the population ecology school focused on. Because it "downgrades the influence of actors' interventions", "the population ecology perspective has been criticized for environmental determinism and the loss of human agency" (Reed, 1992: 137-41; Chong; also see Morgan, 1990: 166-8). The general and all-pervading presumption that organisations follow the instructions of organisers manifests itself everywhere, for instance in our attempts to make sense of organisations that seem 'out of control'. When we feel that an organisation does not do what we want it to do, we do not conclude that organisations are *fundamentally* uncontrollable. Instead we argue that perhaps we are *no longer* in control, for instance because we failed to notice that the organisation has simply grown too big to be managed like a start-up firm. Or because our ideas on how to place an organisation under control are out-of-date. Or because we did not see that changes in the environment demand a completely different organising style. In each of these scenarios, *because* we assume that organisations are essentially manageable, we believe that the problem of 'organisation on the loose' can be fixed. We can try to regain control over the organisation that broke adrift or, better yet, we could have prevented the organisation from slipping out of our hands in the first place – through the dedication of more management hands to handle the expanding organisation, through the prompt application of modern management tools, through timely response to monitored changes in the business environment, and so on.

## Lives of Their Own

As said, this book reflects on an 'urge' to question the primacy of human agency that pervades our thinking of organisation and which leads us to think that in principle and ultimately, organisations are what we want them to be and do what we tell them to do. Using complexity science to develop the opposite idea that organisations live their own lives is not a very straightforward enterprise. For one thing, there is no single answer to the question of what organisations come to look like when we reinterpret them through the discourse of complexity. While some authors maintain that applying complexity to organisations automatically renders the latter systems, others are not convinced that using concepts like self-organisation or emergence requires a commitment to systems thinking. Theorising organisational aliveness is also not easy because of the problematic nature of the signs of organisational life. Especially because we normally do not think of organisations as living entities, there are no apparent indicators of their aliveness. But even if there *was* overall agreement on the features that determine organisational aliveness, then organisations could still not be *proven* to live lives of their own. I argued there is little reason to assume that the properties we find typical of organisations have always been 'out there' as inherent properties of organisation. I believe instead that we *attribute* properties to organisations and only time can tell if these features will come to be *accepted* as real features of organisations. My research needs to be understood as an attempt to partake in the 'programme' of demonstrating organisational aliveness by attributing complexity science informed features of aliveness to organisation.

In chapter 3 I looked at how complexity theory can be used to develop the idea that organisations can learn. While the notion of organisational learning itself is not a new one, in "mainstream" attempts to develop it, "the organizational level cannot avoid dependency on the individual for knowledge generation" (Stacey, 2001: 25). Thinking of organisations as complex systems can help overcome this 'problem'. I argued that students of organisation may benefit from the finding in neural network research that the brain is capable of learning, in spite of the fact that it consists of large numbers of 'stupid' neurons only. If we apply this line of thought to organisation, it follows that the learning capacity of an organisation does not depend on the intelligence of employees but is rather a function of the interactions between system and environment. In this complexity science informed approach to organisational learning, the conventional image of storing information so that it can be called into memory later makes way for a view in which learning takes the form of changes in the very structure of the organisation.

In the chapters 4 and 5 it was argued that when we understand organisation as an emergent phenomenon, it can no longer be thought of as the product of purposeful design and construction. Instead, an organisation becomes a process – not a thing – that emerges from the complicity between the "potential organisation" (defined as the sum of organisational elements) and the "Make-an-Organisation Kit" (the cultural matrix that shapes organisations in the image of other, normal organisations). When we accept that a real organisation is both more than the stuff it is made of *and* more than an expression of the Make-an-Organisation Kit, reductionism loses explanatory power, forcing the science of organisation to extend its methodology to encompass a theory of emergence. I argued that emerging organisations feed themselves back into the sources from which they sprung. The fact that in this process, organisations "change that which brings them about" can be accepted as 'evidence' that organisations live lives of their own.

## Concluding Remarks

When one develops the idea of organisational aliveness in contradistinction to the anthropocentric organisation-as-tool view, one inevitably runs the risk of creating a dichotomy in which either man is alive and organisation his lifeless instrument or the organisation lives its own life and man stops being relevant altogether. An 'either/or' discussion is not in place here, however. While I have used ideas and concepts from the complexity discourse to challenge the presumption that organisation is a derivative of organiser, it has not been my goal to murder human agency as such.

In chapter 3 I argued that thinking of Vitesse president Karel Aalbers as a part of a system rather than as the master of an instrument has important consequences for the relationship between Aalbers and the Vitesse organisation. When Aalbers goes from being *on top of* an organisation to finding himself *in it*, he can no longer be said have a bird's eye perspective on the Vitesse organisation, overseeing the 'big picture' in its totality. From an organisation-as-complex-system point of view, Aalbers has local knowledge only and is thus ignorant of the behaviour of the system as a whole. What is true for Aalbers applies to other elements just the same of course: they too can only respond to the information that is locally available to them. Aalbers' inability to assert his influence 'organisationwide' seriously limits his control over the Vitesse organisation. Understood as a complex system, the behaviour of the Vitesse organisation does not reflect the will of the Vitesse president but is instead defined by system-environment relations and the complex patterns of relationships that emerge from interactions between system elements. By claiming that an organisation is a "perpetuating pattern" in which "no node has any specific significance", the organisation-as-complex-system view does not revolve around man, at least not in the way that the organisation-as-tool view does. However, to argue that people are incapable of fully determining the behaviour of organisations is not the same as to claim that human agency is irrelevant altogether. The same line of argument applies when we understand organisations as emergent phenomena; even when the organisation is not the product of deliberate design but instead emerges from the complicity of processes that no one has control over, man's actions do not become meaningless as such – Aalbers still matters in the emergence of the Vitesse organisation. But again, precisely what role he plays and what his contribution is to the overall behaviour of the Vitesse organisation is impossible to determine.

My attempt to develop a complexity science informed understanding of organisation is perhaps a call for modesty then, more than anything else. I do not think of the discourse of complexity as a source for extending or improving the managerial apparatus. Rather I see concepts like self-organisation, emergence or nonlinearity as indicators of the limits to our ability to put organisations under control. To illustrate what I mean by this I briefly return to the organisation-as-tool view, but only so to rethink the nature of tools. In this book, the concept of tool was deliberately used to invoke the image of a lifeless thing, a dead object that we can use at will. The question of whether or not man really *is* in control of his instruments (in more general terms: technique) has been subject to much debate, however. Belgian philosopher Gilbert Hottois' take on this matter is very similar to my understanding of the relationship between organisers and organisations. Via authors who had already argued that technical and technological developments are largely autonomous and who therefore rejected the anthropocentric and instrumental approach to technique, Hottois (1995) seeks to escape the dichotomy in which one either subjects technique or is subjected by it. Hottois understands the relationship between man and technique as one of interaction and negotiation. That is to say, while Hottois denies that we are capable of fully controlling technical and technological advancements, he does not argue that these advancements withdraw themselves from human intervention completely: we can still guide the developments, accompany them and try to influence their trajectories. In the same vein, our inability to impose our will on organisation does not leave us at the mercy of autonomously operating and developing organisations. But it does mean that there are very real limits to the extent to which we can design, construct, and control organisations. And that, on its turn, has far-reaching implications for the relation between us and the world we try to handle with our organisations.

# Notes

1   Miermans (1955: 145) shows that already in the early years of football, not everyone was convinced that the coarseness of the game could be blamed on the popularisation of football. Even prior to its falling into the hands of the common man, the lofty spirit of gentlemanlike football appeared difficult to uphold. There are various reports on "very unpleasant incidents", such as the home crowd's discourteous treatment of the visiting team or the ridiculing and insulting of the referee. In the year 1900, a football match in Rotterdam was discontinued because of the "less than suitable behaviour" of the spectators (Miermans, 1955: 145).

2   Miermans suspects that the "crusade against professionalism" originated from less enlightened reasons than the ones uttered in public (1955: 189-194). In numerous speeches the KNVB pictured an energetic lad who had no other motive for liking football than wanting to have a good time. This youngster was only able to play football because of the unselfishness of volunteers who dedicated their spare time to 'youth welfare work'. Understood as such, the energy and time these volunteers invested, far from being wasted, was used for the general good and was thus praiseworthy. If football players were in it for the money, on the other hand, the cherished reputation of altruistic well-doers would no longer hold.

3   Apart from Vitesse (1998) and parts of the Vitesse website, all sources on Vitesse are in Dutch and have been translated to English.

4   Aalbers refers to the consequences of the 'Bosman ruling' in particular here. This ruling puts strong limits on the highness of transfer money.

5   This can, in fact, also be formally realised at the Disney Institute "if you're considering benchmarking the Disney Approach to business success". The institute offers programs such as The Disney Approach to Loyalty, The Disney Approach to Leadership Excellence or The Disney Approach to Managing for Creativity & Innovation. See Disney Institute website.

6   Aalbers used the concept of Vitesseworld to refer to the community he imagined would emerge from the effectuation of the Vitesse Way (see Van Mierlo, 2001: 16).

7   Vitesse's mission statement is a confidential text and can therefore not be reviewed in detail. The discussion is limited to those aspects of the mission statement that Vitesse openly communicated.

8   Vitesse considered its organisation chart still 'under construction'. It is therefore not included in the text.

9   N. Katherine Hayles basically sees Kauffman's research programme as a prolongation of that of Wiener's. She understands Kauffman's complexity science as "third wave of cybernetics", the second wave of cybernetics being associated with authors such as Maturana and Varela and their work on autopoiesis (Hayles, 1999: 10-11).

10  For more detailed discussions on the 'problematic' nature of system boundaries see e.g. Cilliers (2001); Midgley, Munlo and Brown (1998: 468); or Stacey (2001: 164-6).

11  The analyses in this chapter are derived from Van Mierlo's (2001) detailed report on the "explosive relationship" between Vitesse and Nuon. Quotes from alternative sources are mentioned explicitly.

12  See Butler (1993) for a critique of the idea that we can safely assume the existence of pre-cultured, "natural" human bodies.

# Bibliography

Ajax prospectus (1998) *Introductiebericht Tevens Prospectus*. Amsterdam: AFC Ajax NV.

Axelrod, R. and M. Cohen (2001) *Complexiteit in organisaties: een raamwerk voor het management*. Amsterdam: Pearson Education Uitgeverij BV.

Bale, L. (1995) 'Gregory Bateson, Cybernetics, and the Social/Behavioral Sciences', *Cybernetics & Human Knowing: A Journal of Second Order Cybernetics & Cyber-Semiotics*, 3(1).

Barthes, R. (1972) *Mythologies*. London: Jonathan Cape Ltd.

Baudrillard, J. (1988) *The Ecstasy of Communication*. Translated by Bernard and Caroline Schutze. New York: Semiotext(e).

Blom, T. (1997) *Complexiteit en Contingentie*. Kampen: Kok Agora.

Boje, D. (1995) 'Stories of the Storytelling Organization: A Postmodern Analysis of Disney as Tamara-land', *Academy of Management Journal*, 38(4): 997-1035.

Borrie, W. (1999) 'Disneyland and Disney World: Constructing the environment, designing the visitor experience', *Loisir et Societe / Society & Leisure*, 22(1): 71-82.

Brailsford, D. (1991) *Sport, Time, and Society: the British at play*. London: Routledge.

Broad, C. (1925) *The Mind and its Place in Nature*. London, UK: Kegan Paul, Trench, Trubner and Co.

Brockman, J. (1995) *The Third Culture: Beyond the Scientific Revolution*. New York: Simon and Schuster.

Burrell, G. (1996) 'Normal Science, Paradigms, Metaphors, Discourses and Genealogies of Analysis', in S. Clegg, C. Hardy and W. Nord (eds), *Handbook of Organization Studies*. London: Sage, pp. 642-658.

Business-Magneet (2002) 'Eenvoudiger Zaken Doen in MiddenOost-Nederland, Complete Informatie Zakelijke Accommodatie Gelredome'. Brochure Vitesse/Gelredome.

Business Plus Magazine (2001) 'Manchester United' at http://www.bizplus.ie/bp_online/companies/?ns=153.

Butler, J. (1993) *Bodies that Matter: On the Discursive Limits of "Sex"*. New York: Routledge.

Butler, J. (1997) *The Psychic Life of Power*. Stanford, California: Stanford University Press.

Byrne, D. (1998) *Complexity and the Social Sciences: An Introduction*. London: Routledge.

Camazine, S., J.-L. Deneubourg, N. Franks, J. Sneyd, G. Theraulaz and E. Bonabeau (eds) (2001) *Self-Organization in Biological Systems*. Princeton, New Jersey: Princeton University Press.

Chia, R. (1995) 'From Modern to Postmodern Organizational Analysis', *Organization Studies*, 16(5): 579-604.

Chia, R. (1996) *Organizational Analysis as Deconstructive Practice*. Berlin: Walter de Gruyter.

Chia, R. (1998) 'From Complexity Science to Complex Thinking: Organization as Simple Location', *Organization*, 5(3): 341-369.

Chong, J. (-) 'Population Ecology' at http://www.stanford.edu/~jchong/articles/quals/Population%20Ecology.doc.

Cilliers, P. (1998) *Complexity and Postmodernism: Understanding Complex Systems*. London: Routledge.

Cilliers, P. (2001) 'Boundaries, Hierarchies and Networks in Complex Systems', *International Journal of Innovation Management*, 5(2): 135-148.

Coffman, B. (1997) 'Weak Signal Research' at http://www.mgtaylor.com/mgtaylor/jotm/winter97/wsrprocm.htm.

Cohen, J. and I. Stewart (1994) *The Collapse of Chaos: Discovering Simplicity in a Complex World*. New York: Penguin Books.

Coleman, H. (1999) 'What Enables Self-Organizing Behavior in Businesses', *Emergence: a Journal of Complexity Issues and Management*, 1(1): 33-48.

Cooper, R. and G. Burrell (1988) 'Modernism, Post Modernism and Organizational Analyses: An Introduction', *Organization Studies*, 9(1): 91-112.

De Geus, A. (1997) *The Living Company: Habits for Survival in a Turbulent Business Environment*. Boston, Massachusetts: Harvard Business School Press.

De Landa, M. (1991) *War in Age of Intelligent Machines*. Cambridge Massachusetts: MIT Press.

De Landa, M. (1997) *A Thousand Years of Nonlinear History*. Cambridge, Massachusetts: MIT Press.

Dialoog (2000) 'De Sponsor in de Stilte na de Storm', *Dialoog: Uitgave van de Beroepsvereniging voor Communicatie*, 5(39): 3-5.

Edelman, G. (1987) *Neural Darwinism: The Theory of Neural Group Selection*. New York: Basic Books.

Eliot, M. (1993) *Walt Disney: Hollywood's Dark Prince*. New York: Birch Lane Press, Carol Publishing.

Emory, C. (2001) 'The Disney Institute Approach to Human Capital: An Interview With Larry Lynch' at http://www.linezine.com/4.1/interviews/llcediahc.htm.

Ferweda, H., B. Beke en A. Van Wijk (1998) *Kwaliteit Op en Rondom het Voetbalveld: Naar een Integrale Aanpak van Onveiligheidsproblemen*. Arnhem: Advies- en Onderzoeksgroep Beke.

Fuller, T. and P. Moran (2000) 'Moving Beyond Metaphor', *Emergence: a Journal of Complexity Issues and Management*, 2(1): 50-71.

Fulmer, W. (2000) *Shaping the Adaptive Organisation: Landscapes, Learning and Leadership in Volatile Times*. New York: Amacom.

Garfinkel, A. (1987) 'The Slime Mold *Dyctyostelium* as a Model of Self-Organization in Social Systems', in F. Yates (ed), *Self-Organizing Systems: The Emergence of Order*. New York: Plenum Press, pp. 181-212.

Gergen, K. (1992) 'Organization Theory in the Postmodern Era', in M. Reed and M. Hughes (eds), *Rethinking organization*. London: Sage, pp. 206-226.

Grandori, A. (1987) *Perspectives on Organization Theory*. Cambridge, Massachusetts: Ballinger.

Griffin, D. (2002) *The Emergence of Leadership: Linking Self-Organization and Ethics*. London: Routledge.

Hannigan, J. (1998) *Fantasy City: Pleasure and Profit in the Postmodern Metropolis*. New York: Routledge.

Hardison, O. (1989) *Disappearing through the Skylight: Culture and Technology in the Twentieth Century*. New York: Viking.

Hayles, N. Katherine (1993) 'The Materiality of Informatics', *Configurations*, 1(1): 147-170.

Hayles, N. Katherine (1999) *How We Became Posthuman: Virtual Bodies in Cybernetics, Literature, and Informatics*. Chicago: University of Chicago Press.

Hayles, N. Katherine (1999a) 'From Chaos to Complexity: Moving Through Metaphor to Practice' at http://www.southernct.edu/chaos-nursing/chaos4.htm.

Hayles, N. Katherine (2000), 'Making the Cut', in W. Rasch, and C. Wolfe (eds), *Observing Complexity*. Minnesota: University of Minnesota Press, pp 137-162.

Holliss, R. and B. Sibley (1988) *The Disney Story*. London: Octopus Books.

Hottois, G. (1995) *Symbool en Techniek*. Kampen: Kok Agora.

Irvin, L. (2002) 'Ethics in Organizations: a Chaos Perspective', *Journal of Organizational Change Management*, 15(4): 359-381.

Hout, T. (1999) 'Are Managers Obsolete?', *Harvard Business Review*, March-April: 161-168.

James, K. (1999) Quoted from unpublished transcripts proceedings, *Managing the Complex Conference*, Boston, Massachusetts.

Jeffcutt, P. (1989) *Persistence and Change in an Organisation Culture*. Unpublished PhD thesis, University of Manchester.

Jeffcutt, P. (1993) 'From Interpretation to Representation', in J. Hassard, and M. Parker (eds), *Postmodernism and Organizations*. London: Sage, pp.25-48.

Johnson, J. and B. Burton (1994) 'Chaos and Complexity Theory for Management: Caveat Emptor', *Journal of Management Inquiry*, 3(4): 320-328.

Joslyn, C. and L. Rocha (2000) 'Towards Semiotic Agent-Based Models of Socio-Technical Organizations' in H. Sarjoughian et al (eds) Proceedings AI, *Simulation and Planning in High Autonomy Systems* (AIS 2000) Conference, Tucson, Arizona: pp. 70-79.

Juarrero, A. (1999) *Dynamics in Action: Intentional Behavior as a Complex System*. Cambridge, Massachusetts: The MIT Press.

Katz, D. and R. Kahn (1966) *The Social Psychology of Organizations*. New York: John Wiley & Sons.

Kauffman, S. (1995) *At Home in the Universe: The Search for Laws of Self-Organization and Complexity*. Oxford: Oxford University Press.

Kellner, D. (2002) 'The Sports Spectacle, Michael Jordan, and Nike: Unholy Alliance?' at http://www.gseis.ucla.edu/faculty/kellner/kellner.html.

Kelly, S. and M. Allison (1999) *The Complexity Advantage: How the Science of Complexity can Help your Business Achieve Peak Performance.* New York: McGraw-Hill.

Koenig, D. (1994) *Mouse Tales: A Behind-The-Ears Look at Disneyland.* Irving, California: Bonaventure Press.

Kopicki, L. (2001) Report on Business Internship at Walt Disney World Resort at http://fieryangel.diaryland.com/011204_77.html.

Krogh, C. (1996) 'The Rights of Agents', in M. Wooldridge, J. Muller and M. Tambe (eds), *Intelligent Agents II: Agent Theories, Architectures and Languages.* Heidelberg: Springer Verlag.

Kroker, A. and M. Kroker (1987) 'Thesis on the Disappearing Body in the Hyper-modern Condition' in A. Kroker and M. Kroker (eds), *Body Invaders: Panic Sex in America.* New York: St. Martin's Press, pp 20-34.

Levy, D., M. Alvesson, and H. Willmott (1999) 'Critical Approaches to Strategic Management', paper presented at the Critical Management Studies Conference, hosted by the Manchester School of Management, July 14-16.

Lewin, R. (1993) *Complexity: Life on the Edge of Chaos.* London: Phoenix.

Lewin, R. and B. Regine (2000) *The Soul at Work: Unleashing the Power of Complexity Science for Business Success.* London: Orion Business Books.

Letiche, H. (2000) 'Phenomenal Complexity Theory as Informed by Bergson', *Journal of Organizational Change Management,* 13(6): 545-557.

Letiche, H. and J. van Uden (1998) 'Answers to a Discussion Note: On the Metaphor of Metaphor', *Organization Studies,* 19(6): 1029-1033.

Lissack, M. (1999), 'Complexity: the Science, its Vocabulary, and its Relation to Organizations', *Emergence: a Journal of Complexity Issues and Management,* 1(1): 110-126.

Lissack, M. and H. Gunz (1999) *Managing Complexity in Organizations: a View in Many Directions.* Westport, Connecticut: Quorum Books.

Lissack, M. and J. Roos (1999) *The Next Common Sense.* London: Nicholas Brealey Publishing Ltd.

Maguire, S. and B. McKelvey (1999), 'Complexity and Management: Moving from Fad to Firm Foundations', *Emergence: a Journal of Complexity Issues and Management,* 1(2): 19-61.

Marion, R. and J. Bacon (1999), 'Organizational Extinctions and Complex Systems', *Emergence: a Journal of Complexity Issues and Management,* 1(4): 71-96.

Marling, K. (1997) 'Imagineering the Disney Theme Parks', K. Marling (ed), *Designing Disney's Theme Parks: The Architecture of Reassurance.* New York: Flammarion.

Marin. L. (1983) 'Disneyland: A Degenerate Utopia' in S. Weber and H. Sussman (eds), *Glyph One: Textual Studies.* Baltimore, Maryland: John Hopkins University Press.

McKelvey, B. (1999) 'Complexity Theory in Organization Science: Seizing the Promise or Becoming a Fad', *Emergence: a Journal of Complexity Issues and Management,* 1(1): 5-33.

McNeal, J. (1992) *Kids as Customers: A Handbook of Marketing to Children*. New York: Lexington Books.

Medd, W. and P. Haynes (1998) 'Complexity and the Social' at http://www.keele.ac.uk/depts/stt/cstt2/comp/medd.htm.

Meiss, J. (2000), 'sci.nonlinear faq' at http://amath.colorado.edu/faculty/jdm/faq.html.

Menzies Jones, H. (1996) 'Confessions of an Upstate New York Mother: Disney World' at http://www.chem.rochester.edu/~jones/hmj/.

Michael, K., C. Michael and G. Rebecca (1999) 'Why Study the Complexity Sciences in the Social Sciences', *Human Relations* 52(4): 439-642.

Midgley, G., I. Munlo and M. Brown (1998) 'The Theory and Practice of Boundary Critique: Developing Housing Services for Older People', *Journal of Operational Research Society*, 49: 467-478.

Miermans, C. (1955) *Voetbal in Nederland: Maatschappelijke en Sportieve Aspecten*. Assen: Van Gorcum.

Mikulecky, D. (1995) 'Life, Complexity and the Edge of Chaos: Cognitive Aspects of Communication Between Cells and other Components of Living Systems' at http://views.vcu.edu/~mikuleck/rev.htm.

Mikulecky, D. (2000) 'A Close Look at a New Science: Chaos as Science or Science in Chaos?' at http://views.vcu.edu/~mikuleck/chaos2.htm.

Miller, D. (1957) *Disney: The story of Walt Disney (as told to Pete Martin)*. New York: Dell.

Marion, R. (1999) *The Edge of Organization: Chaos and Complexity Theories of Formal Social Systems*. London: Sage.

Moravec, H. (1988) *Mind Children: The Future of Robot and Human Intelligence*. Cambridge, Massachusetts: Harvard University Press.

Morgan, G. (1980) 'Paradigms, Metaphors, and Puzzle Solving in Organization Theory', *Administrative Science Quarterly*, 25(4): 605-622.

Morgan, G. (1983) 'More on metaphor: Why We Cannot Control Tropes in Administrative Science', *Administrative Science Quarterly*, 28(4): 601-607.

Morgan, G. (1986) *Images of Organization*, Newbury Park, California: Sage Publications.

Morgan G. (1990) *Organizations in Society*. London: MacMillan.

Maturana, H. and F. Varela (1987) *The Tree of Knowledge: The Biological Roots of Human Understanding*. Boston, Massachusetts: Shambhala Publications

Nietzsche, F. (1872) *Philosophenbuch*, translated in D. Breazeale (1979) *Philosophy and Truth: Selections from Nietzsche's Notebooks of the Early 1870s*. Sussex, New Jersey: Humanities Press, pp.50-1.

Olson, E. and G. Eoyang (2001) *Facilitating Organization Change: Lessons from Complexity Science*. San Fransico, California: John Wiley & Sons.

Organise! (1999) 'Disneyfication or Nostalgia ain't what it used to be' in *Organise! for Revolutionary Anarchism*, issue 51 at http://burn.ucsd.edu/~acf/org/issue51/.

Ott, J. (1989) *The Organizational Culture Perspective*. Pacific Grove, California: Brooks/Cole.

Phelan, S. (1999) 'A Note on the Correspondence Between Complexity and Systems Theory' at http://www.utdallas.edu/~sphelan/Papers/systems.html.

Reed, M. (1992) *The Sociology of Organizations: Themes, Perspectives and Prospects.* London: Harvester Wheatsheaf.

Regine, B. and R. Lewin (2000) 'Leading at the Edge: How Leaders Influence Complex Systems' in *Emergence: a Journal of Complexity Issues and Management* 2(2): 5-23.

Sanders, I. (1998) *Strategic Thinking and the New Science: Planning in the Midst of Chaos, Complexity, and Change.* New York: Free Press.

Schein, E. (1985) *Organizational Culture and Leadership.* San Francisco, California: Jossey-Bass.

Senesac, L. (1995) 'Complexity is in the Eye of the Beholder' at http://aurora.phys.utk.edu/~senesac/Complexity.html.

Senge, P. (1990) *The Fifth Discipline: The Art and Practice of the Learning Organization.* New York: Doubleday.

Shaw, P. (2002) *Changing Conversations in Organizations: a Complexity Approach to Change.* London: Routledge.

Stacey, R. (1996) *Complexity and Creativity in Organizations.* San Francisco, California: Berrett-Koehler.

Stacey, R. (2001) *Complex Responsive Processes in Organizations.* London: Routledge.

Stewart I. and J. Cohen (1997) *Figments of Reality.* Cambridge: Cambridge University Press.

Stokvis, R. (1979) *Strijd over Sport: Organisatorische en Ideologische Ontwikkelingen.* Deventer: Van Loghum Slaterus.

Streatfield, P. (2001) *The Paradox of Control in Organizations.* London: Routledge

Stuever, H. (2001) 'America Loves to Hate the Mouse: Behind the Fantasy Walt Disney Built Looms a Dark Reality. On His 100th Anniversary, It Can Now Be Revealed', article in the Washington Post, December 5: pp C01.

Styhre, A., A. Ingelgard and J. Roth (2000), 'A Nonreductionist View of Knowledge: Product Development in the Pharmaceutical Industry', *Emergence: a Journal of Complexity Issues and Management* 2(3): 51-67.

Svyantek, D. and Brown, L. (2001) 'Stability in the American Automobile Industry', *Emergence: a Journal of Complexity Issues and Management*, 3(3): 42-57.

Van Maanen, J. (1991) *The Smile Factory: Work at Disneyland*, in P. Frost, L. Moore, M. Louis, C. Lundberg, and J. Martin (eds), Reframing organizational culture. Newbury Park, California: Sage, pp. 58-76.

Van Maanen, J. (1992) 'Displacing Disney: Some Notes on the Flow of Culture', *Qualitative Sociology*, 15(1): 5-35.

Van Mierlo, J. (2001) *Verspeelde Energie: Vitesse en NUON, Verslag van een Explosieve Relatie.* Nijmegen: SUN.

Van Nijnatten, C. (-) 'Vitesse Heeft Karel Aalbers Nodig', *Voetbal International*, date unknown.

Van Pelt, T. (2000) 'Otherness', *Postmodern Culture* 10(2).

Vanderbilt, T. (1999) 'It's a Mall World After All', *Harvard Design Magazine* (Fall, nr. 9)

Verkammen, M and E. Vermeer (1994) *Om het Spel en de Knikkers, 40 Jaar Betaald Voetbal in Nederland.* Bilthoven: Mundt Print en Bookmarketing.

Vitesse (1998) *Gelredome: a visions realised, an innovation by Vitesse professional football foundation.* Arnhem: Rood & Partners.

Waldrop, M. (1992) *Complexity: The Emerging Science at the Edge of Order and Chaos.* London: Simon & Schuster.

Werken aan Werk (1998) Documentary '*Vitesse*', broadcasted by RVU Educatieve Omroep.

Wheatley, M. (1993) *Leadership and the New Science.* San Francisco, California: Berrett-Koehler.

Wiener, N. (1948) *Cybernetics, or Control and Communication in the Animal and the Machine.* Cambridge, Massachusetts: MIT Press.

Wiener, N. (1954) *The Human Use of Human Beings: Cybernetics and Society*, 2nd ed. New York: Garden City.

Wood, R. (1999) 'The Future of Strategy: The Role of the New Sciences' in M. Lissack and H. Gunz (eds), *Managing Complexity in Organizations: a View in Many Directions.* Westport, Connecticut: Quorum Books, pp. 118-159.

Young, T. (1990) 'Chaos and the Drama of Social Change: A Metaphysic for Postmodern Science', distributed as part of *Transforming Sociology Series* of The Red Feather Institute at http://www.tryoung.com/archives/147chaos&socialchange.html.

Youngblood, M. (1997) *Life at the Edge of Chaos: Creating the Quantum Organization.* Dallas, Texas: Perceval Publishing.

Zeleny, M. (1996) 'On the Social Nature of Autopoietic Systems', in E. Khalil and K. Boulding (eds), *Evolution, Order and Complexity.* London: Routledge.

## WEBSITES

*Ajax*, website at www.ajax.nl

*Consumers Union*, website at www.consunion.org/other/sellingkids/kidsclubs.htm

*Disney*, website at www.disney.com

*Disney Alumni*, website at www.disneyalumni.com/info/handbook

*Euronext*, website at www.euronext.nl

*Greenpeace*, website at www.greenpeace.org/history/

*Greenpeace USA*, website at www.greenpeaceusa.org/inside/

*Unilever*, website at www.unilever.com

*Vitesse*, website at www.vitesseworld.nl. This site is no longer in use. The contents of the new official Vitesse website www.vitesse.nl have been changed, which means that texts to which reference is made may not be available anymore.

Printed in the United States
210081BV00006BA/221-224/A

9 781581 12221